Easy-to-Build

Model Railroad Structures

EDITED BY WILLARD V. ANDERSON

Managing Editor of MODEL RAILROADER

KALMBACH BOOKS

First printing, 1958. Second printing, 1960. Third printing, 1963. Fourth printing, 1968. Fifth printing, 1971. Sixth printing, 1973. Seventh printing, 1976.

A WORD ABOUT THIS BOOK

A MODEL RAILROAD is more than locomotives and cars and track. To be truly representative of the real thing, a model railroad must also have buildings — stations, enginehouses, section houses and the like. To round out the scene and give the railroad a job to do, the layout should also include lineside industries.

Easy-to-Build Model Railroad Structures is a collection of construction articles from past issues of the old MODEL TRAINS. From it you can choose various types of structures best suited to your own needs, and build them from scratch. Some of the items are very similar to some that are available in kit form, if you prefer to build from kits.

For your convenience, scale rules for N, HO, S, and O scales are included in the margins of this page and pages 2, 3 and 4. To build in any scale, measure the drawings with the rule which matches the scale of the drawings; then measure your work with the rule for your gauge. Because HO scale is used by more people than any other, most of the drawings, but not all of them, are given in HO scale.

All these structures are in this book!
Pages are indicated by circled numbers

CONTENTS

INDEX OF AUTHORS

Empire Station is a neatly detailed structure, complete with a bay window.

Small-town station

BY JOE WILHELM   **Illustrated by the author**

Easy-to-Build Model Railroad Structures

PART 1: STATIONS
Freight and passenger

SEVERAL years ago, in the pages of the old *HO Monthly* magazine, I described some of the rolling stock of the narrow-gauge Buffalo River & Empire RR., which was HOn3. The great BR&E went the way of all good model railroads — it was torn up to make space for the super-colossal railroad of my dreams. The only drawback was that it takes a lot more than dreams to build a super-duper pike, so until now the BR&E has existed only in my head.

Now, however, I have begun construction on the new BR&E. Instead of the huge railroad I dreamed of, however, it will be one of modest proportions. I have learned over the years that it is a mistake to attempt too much, for you never get finished, and work when attempted in quantity never has the quality desired. So this new road will be small, but I hope it will be something to be proud of.

The new BR&E is HO standard gauge, so I sold all my narrow-gauge equipment. I have planned a new group of structures, all built to the same style of architecture. Empire Station, shown here, is one of them. It is easy to build and very attractive. Perhaps you'd like one for your road.

Construction

I used balsa wood, acetate and paper to make this station. Northeastern siding works fine, if you want to use it. In Fig. 1, you can see the front, rear and side elevations. Study these carefully. Fig. 3 shows the station in relation to the track.

Cut out the sides and ends using 1/32″ sheet balsa or the Northeastern sid-

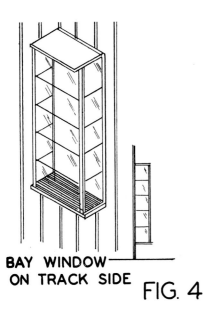

BAY WINDOW
ON TRACK SIDE
FIG. 4

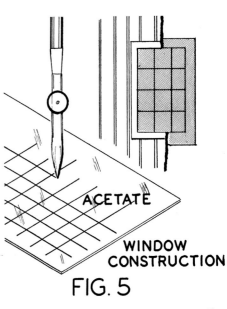

ACETATE

WINDOW
CONSTRUCTION
FIG. 5

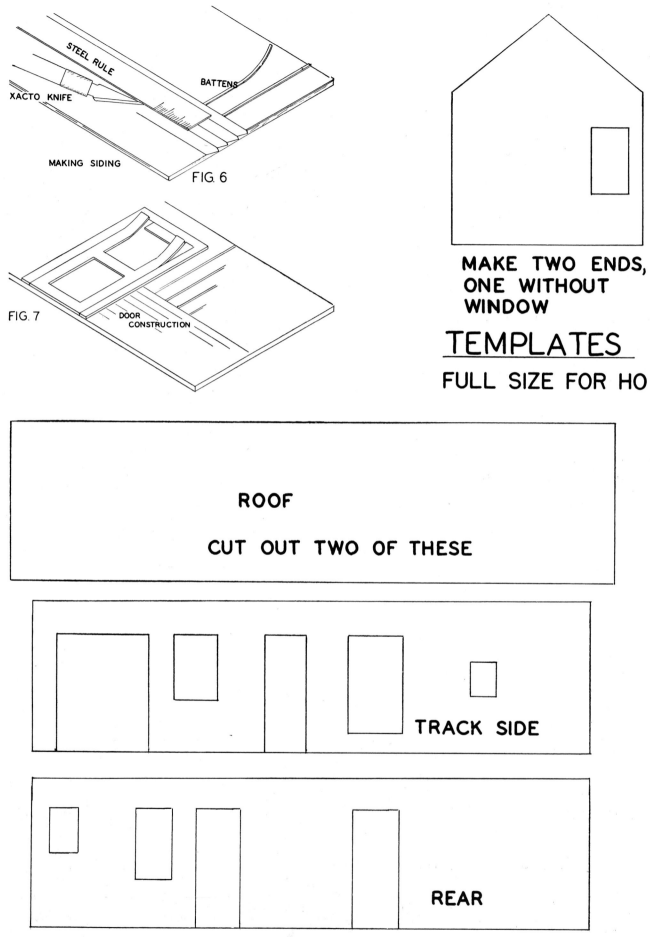

STEEL RULE

BATTENS

XACTO KNIFE

MAKING SIDING

FIG. 6

FIG. 7   DOOR CONSTRUCTION

MAKE TWO ENDS, ONE WITHOUT WINDOW

TEMPLATES

FULL SIZE FOR HO

ROOF

CUT OUT TWO OF THESE

TRACK SIDE

REAR

FIG. 2

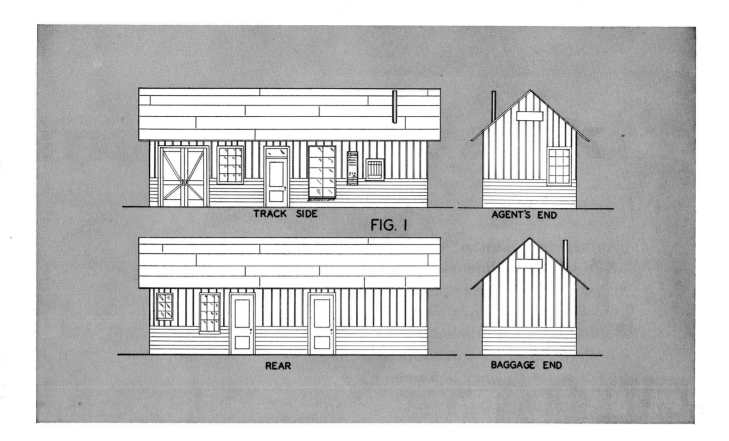

TRACK SIDE   FIG. 1   AGENT'S END

REAR   BAGGAGE END

ing. Use the templates in Fig. 2 for these parts. Cut two pieces for the two sides of the roof, using the one template shown.

If you use sheet balsa for the structure, Fig. 6 shows how the siding is made. The battens are little slivers of balsa glued in place. Make the weatherboarding with an X-acto knife by pressing, not cutting, the indentations. Use a 6″ steel rule as a guide; with a little practice, you'll be able to do this rapidly. If you intend to have the doors in a closed position, do not cut the openings for them. Simply build up the molding right on the solid side. See Fig. 7 for this step.

Construct the windows as in Fig. 5. If you have never tried this method, you will be pleased at the results. Use Testors dope in a ruling pen to draw on the mullions. The bay window is a little more difficult to do, and if you wish you can omit it entirely. It is supposed to let the station agent see up and down the track without going outside. You can see its construction in Fig. 4.

Cut a floor piece to the inside dimensions of the sides and ends. When this is glued inside, it will strengthen the building quite a bit and prevent any buckling of the sides at a later date.

I painted my station yellow and red, with a black tarpaper roof. The tarpaper is simulated by gluing strips of paper on the balsa roof. The little stovepipe is of metal tubing, glued and braced from the inside.

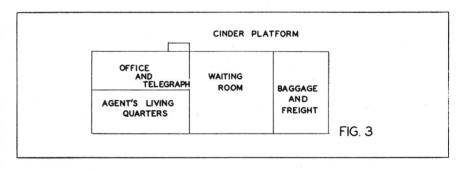

TRACK

CINDER PLATFORM

OFFICE
AND
TELEGRAPH

WAITING
ROOM

BAGGAGE
AND
FREIGHT

AGENT'S LIVING
QUARTERS

FIG. 3

Windows, doors, siding and weatherboarding show the results of careful work.

Old-time Station

BY BILL LAWRENCE JR.

HERE is a structure that will fit right in with those old diamond-stacked wood burners and open-end coaches. Stations such as this were built back in the '80's and '90's, and many of them are still in use on branch lines today. The filigree around the eaves of this structure places it chronologically at about the turn of the century.

The station is easily built from bristol board with cardboard overlays around the windows and doors, or from Northeastern's capped siding.

The roof can be covered either with commercial roof paper or a very fine grade of black emery paper to simulate tar paper. Both are quite effective. The black emery paper has a little sparkle to it that catches the eye.

The fancy ironwork is a design cut from paper doilies, which can be obtained in a five-and-ten store. Ten or 20 cents' worth of it will last you for years. After it is painted it becomes quite stiff and will withstand considerable handling. Try to get the square-type doily rather than the

oval and you will save yourself a lot of cutting and fitting.

The leaders from the gutters are copper bell wire bent and cemented in place. If you have rain barrels handy you can place one under each drain for added realism.

One suggestion if you are going to construct the station from cardboard: Be sure to brace each side well with square balsa wood strips to prevent any warping or buckling. Other than that, the construction is the same as that of any other structure.

Photos above show a front view of the old-time station at the top and a back view at the bottom, while at the left are HO-scale drawings of the front and side. Fancy ironwork on the roof was designed to stop snow slides.

Dimensions given in sketch are for HO scale. To build the model in O scale, multiply by 2 and subtract 10 per cent. For S scale, multiply by 1½ and subtract 10 per cent.

Southern Railway *Ties.*

The prototype for the author's log station stood at Jarrets (now Nantahala), N. C., on the Southern's Murphy Branch.

FROM LOG CABIN DAYS

BY ROBERT E. GILBERT

A backwoods station

Robert E. Gilbert.

A connecting platform runs from the passenger station to the freight house. Remove the bark from sticks and twigs before cutting "logs" for construction.

IN the September 1955 issue of the Southern Railway System's magazine *Ties,* I found the most rustic old-time station I've seen. The picture showed two log buildings at what is now Nantahala, N. C., a town about 10 miles below the southern boundary of Great Smoky Mountains National Park. The group seemed a correct prototype for my Razorback-East Grimalkin Ry. (HO) and I decided to model it.

You can probably use a log station on your layout; although the prototype photograph was taken in 1896, the style of architecture is suitable for almost any railroading period, from

FRONT

PASSENGER STATION   FREIGHT HOUSE

BACK

the pioneer days of 1830 to the present. Such a station might be found today on a branch line — possibly abandoned — or it might be restored as a railroad museum. The passenger station alone can double as a log cabin.

With the exception of some thicknesses which are for HO, the dimensions on the plans are in scale feet to accommodate any gauge. The first step is to acquire sticks and twigs for logs. The walls of my model are ordinary hedge, 6 to 12 scale inches in diameter; seasoned and with the bark removed. Other twigs, especially evergreens, may be suitable. Avoid twigs with pithy centers. If you can't easily obtain natural wood, use dowels of several sizes; whittle them a bit to make them look more like logs.

The drawings at the right illustrate the method of cutting logs, while the one labeled "passenger station parts" on page 13 gives the types required. Because of different diameters, the number of logs required may vary from one model to another. No exact figure for the height of the walls can be given. The height of the front wall of the passenger station is the height of the door frame plus the thicknesses of two logs.

Use a sharp pocket knife for log carving, because a thinner blade may break. First, cut the principal 13-foot logs with two notches at each end.

1. MARK LENGTH.

2. ROLL AND CUT.

3. CUT TO DEPTH OF NOTCHES.

4. CUT NOTCHES.

5. FINISHED LOG.

CARVING LOGS FROM TWIGS

LOG RAISING
(PASSENGER STATION)

On your workbench or cutting board, mark spaces of 6", 12", 10'-0", 12" and 6". Using these lines as a guide, mark twigs until you have measured off about 20 logs. By pressing the knife into the twig and rolling it, cut off the 13-foot logs. Carve 12"-wide notches 6" away from each end on the top and bottom of each log. Cut four logs with only one notch at each end.

Make the other logs called for in a similar manner; keep the various sizes separated. On the smaller ones you may find it easier to whittle the notches before cutting the logs from the twigs.

Cut the floor for the passenger station from a piece of ⅛"-thick balsa or other wood; it is 10 feet square. For extra detail, scribe slightly crooked lines, about a foot apart, to imitate a floor of puncheons, which are logs split in half.

I cut the pieces for the door frame from 1⁄32" balsa sheet, but you may prefer wood strips. Make the inner frame an open box of 12" planks, measuring 2'-6" x 6'-6" inside. Cement the four pieces together, keeping the corners square. Add three 6" planks for outside trim. Cut the door from 1⁄32" balsa and scribe rough planks. Add a bit of wood for a handle. Cement the door into the frame.

To make the windows, cut two

SIDES

HO SCALE

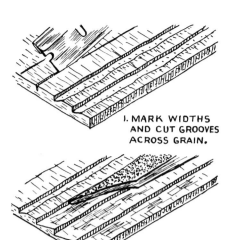

1. MARK WIDTHS AND CUT GROOVES ACROSS GRAIN.

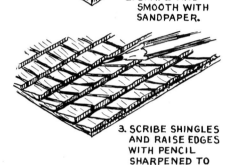

2. SHAPE AND SMOOTH WITH SANDPAPER.

3. SCRIBE SHINGLES AND RAISE EDGES WITH PENCIL SHARPENED TO WEDGE POINT.

CARVING SHINGLES FROM 1/16" THICK BALSA

sashes from card stock; something like a file folder will do. The 3" width given for the mullions is a bit wide, although not especially noticeable in HO. For a larger gauge, you might narrow them. Cement clear acetate or cellophane to the backs of the sashes for glass. Make rectangles of 12" planks for the frames and secure the windows inside.

Study the three sketches above for the method of carving shingles. Balsa, 1/16" thick, is easier to work in this way than a harder wood.

First make the front section of the roof. With the longer dimension across the grain, cut a piece of wood 10 x 15 feet and miter the upper edge slightly for a good fit at assembly. Cement a piece of paper, about 8 x 15 feet, in the center of the back to strengthen the material. Measure down 2'-6" for the overlapping top row of shingles. Mark off the four remaining rows about 22½" wide. Along these lines, carve slightly wavering grooves. Smooth the grooves with sandpaper until the slope is flat.

Run a hard pencil across a piece of sandpaper, sharpening the point to a thin wedge. With this tool, scribe shingles not over a foot wide. Carefully stick the point under the edge of each row, lift up individual shingles, and create the illusion that the roof is not in one piece. You can also indicate the ends of planks at the sides of the roof. For a final touch, turn the section over and at each end lightly cut notches to imitate boards running across the roof on which the shingles are laid.

The back section differs slightly. It is not mitered at the top edge, but has an extra row of shingles that will overhang the front section. There is a 9" x 15" hole for a smoke pipe.

The smoke pipe is a 5-foot length of 3/32" brass or aluminum tubing. Cut the flashing from shim metal or card stock and punch a 9" x 12" hole.

Carving the two gables is similar to making the roof. Cut these parts from 1/8"-thick wood. To indicate overlapping boards split from logs, carve grooves across. Cut a 12"-square notch at either side. On the back, cut a groove 9" square, all the way across, so that the gable will fit over the top log of the side wall. If the bottom plank breaks off at this delicate point, cement it back in place.

The final part for the passenger station is the walk, 4 x 20 feet, that extends across the front of the building and over to the freight house. Scribe a piece of 1/32" wood for the boards. Turn the part over and attach six sup-

ports, 6" x 4'-0", also of 1/32" wood. Make the step that will be against the freight house platform from a timber about 12" square.

Assembling the station

If you have ever owned a toy log set, the experience will be helpful when you begin to assemble your log station. As shown in the drawing on page 11, raising the walls is simply a matter of fitting logs in a square, although doors and windows complicate things slightly.

Fasten the floor to your work surface with pins. Among your piles of logs, you'll find four with notches only on one side. Take two of these and, with the notches on top, cement one to the front edge and one to the back edge of the floor. Then take two 13-foot logs with four notches. Cement them into the notches of the first two logs so that they form the lower courses on the sides of the building. Place another 13-foot log across the back wall.

Cement the door frame and door to the first log in the front wall, keeping it perpendicular to the floor. It should be 2'-9" from one end of the log and 7'-3" from the other. Select a log of each of these dimensions. Smear cement on the sides of the door frame, let it become tacky, and then fasten these two logs in place, one on each side of the frame. If necessary, use small slivers of wood as props in order to maintain the gap between courses of logs.

Continue around the walls, adding one log at a time. Try to keep the logs parallel to the floor, or the building will have some of the corners higher than others. You may have to cement pieces of wood in some notches and cut others deeper to keep the logs level.

Check occasionally so that you'll know when to add the windows. The tops of the window and door frames should be level, or almost level. When this point arrives, cement the back

Both photos, Robert E. Gilbert.

The back view of the station shows how logs are fitted around the window and door. Putty or clay is forced between the cracks from the inside to fill in the gaps.

The side view of both buildings shows how gables are made. Grooves are carved in the wood to look like overlapping boards and bottom plank is notched to fit the logs.

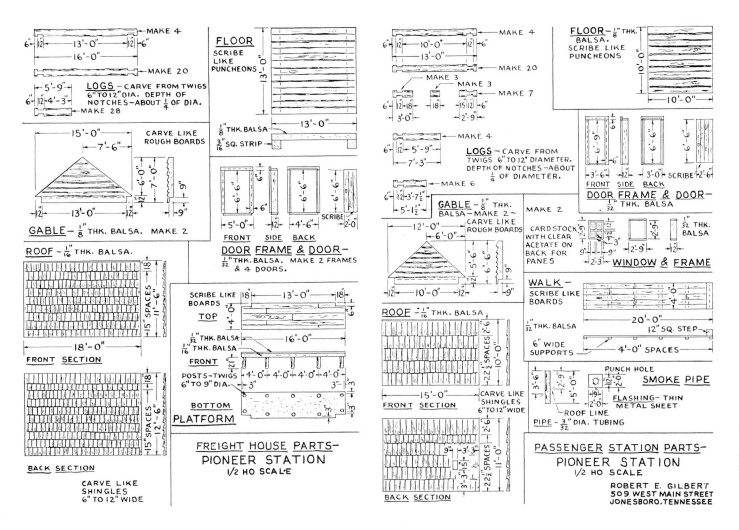

FREIGHT HOUSE PARTS—PIONEER STATION
1/2 HO SCALE

PASSENGER STATION PARTS—PIONEER STATION
1/2 HO SCALE

ROBERT E. GILBERT
509 WEST MAIN STREET
JONESBORO, TENNESSEE

window in the center of a 13-foot log and put a log 5'-1½" long on each side of it. Affix the front window to a log 7'-3" long, and place a 3-foot log on one side of it and an 18" log on the other side.

When the courses of logs have reached to within a few inches of the tops of the door and window frames, and there is one higher log on each side wall, take the two remaining 13-foot logs with only two notches and put one across the front wall, above door and window, and one across the back.

The log raising is now finished, but the walls must be daubed. First, cut two 10-foot poles, about 6" in diameter, and cement them against the exposed edges of the floor under the bottom logs of the side walls. Cut a few pieces of plank from 1/32" wood and insert them at random between logs on all sides of the building.

My model is daubed with Marblex, a self-setting clay. Other materials that might be substituted are putty, Sculp-metal, or ceramic clay. Use a flat modeling tool or strip of wood; coat the walls on the *inside* with clay, but be careful not to smear the windows. Smooth the clay and force it through the gaps between logs. The clay will appear in rounded ridges on

the outside. Flatten these ridges and scrape off any excess clay.

Cement the gables to the side walls with the long groove fitting over the top logs. The notches fit over the front and back walls. If the gables tend to lean inward, you can keep them apart by fitting a strip of wood across the peak.

Attach the front section of the roof with the top of the section flush with the peak. The other three sides overhang the walls about a foot. Add the back section, overlapping the front section at the top. Cement the smoke pipe flashing over the rectangular openings. Insert the pipe, leaving about 3'-6" of its length exposed on the lower side.

Cement the walk to the front wall and your passenger station is complete.

Freight house

When you begin building the freight house you should have no difficulty. Constructing it is mostly repetition of the methods used for the passenger station. A few points should be emphasized, perhaps.

Notice that the 1/8"-thick floor is raised on two 3/16"-square strips to make it about a scale 2'-6" high.

There are double doors that open inward in front and in back of the

station. Put two doors measuring 2'-6" in each frame.

The roof shingles are shorter than those on the passenger station.

To erect the platform, scribe a piece of 1/32" wood, 4 x 16 feet, to resemble planks. Cement it to a piece of 1/16"-thick wood of the same dimensions. Notch the ends to fit around the logs at assembly. Turn this part over, cut 10 posts from twigs about 6" in diameter, and cement them in the positions shown on the plans.

When you assemble the freight house, run two courses of logs across the front and the back before adding the door frames. If possible, have the platform, the inside of the door frames and the floor even. It may be necessary to flatten a place in the center of the logs to do this.

Since most old log buildings are unpainted and weatherbeaten, I stained my models with some much-used thinner that had become an interesting gray. I applied two coats to the walls and three to the roofs, and put touches of mossy green on the bottom logs. I painted the smoke pipe and flashing with box car red and black for a rusty, sooty effect. If yours is a modern railroad, you could paint the buildings a dark creosote brown to preserve them.

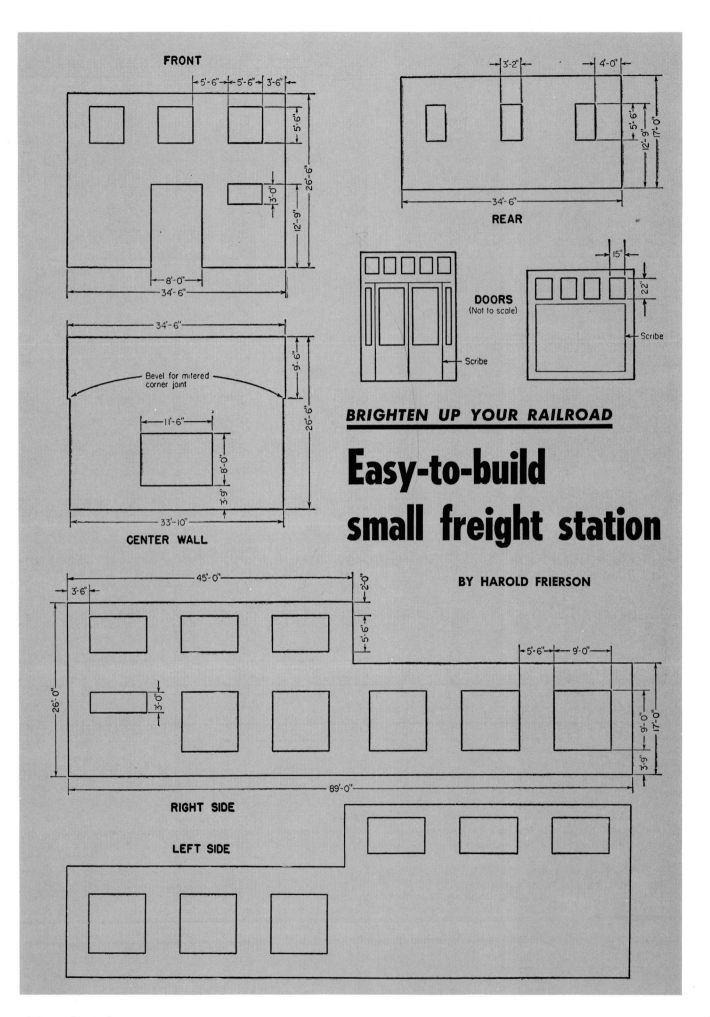

FRONT

REAR

DOORS
(Not to scale)

Scribe

Scribe

Bevel for mitered
corner joint

CENTER WALL

BRIGHTEN UP YOUR RAILROAD

Easy-to-build small freight station

BY HAROLD FRIERSON

RIGHT SIDE

LEFT SIDE

This trim freight station is ready for business. Harold Frierson used Suydam's red brick matboard for the sides, and carefully mitered the corners.

EVERY model trainman strives for color on his layout, and here is a freight station that will enhance the beauty of any medium- or large-size model railroad. You can build it yourself, but be prepared to spend time on it. The necessary tools required are: a heavy cutting knife, a razor blade, a ½" mill file, a No. 2 fine-pointed flat file, scissors, drawing board and draftsman's T square, plus the usual scale rule.

The walls of this building are constructed of E. Suydam & Company's HO gauge red brick matboard. This is one of the finest and prettiest building materials available on the market. It is an embossed high-density matboard nearly $\frac{1}{16}$" thick. The brick and mortar detail are beautiful. The use of brick siding for the walls requires mitered corner joints with inside reinforcing blocks, but this fine matboard will bevel beautifully and you can have perfectly matched corner bricks.

There are 23 openings in this structure for the doors and windows. Using a sharp cutting knife and rule, you can line them up perfectly; then your ½" mill file will clean up any ragged edges and square up the corners. The station I built has pink-red brick walls, coach-green roof, orange-brown doors and trim and casement windows.

Walls and Floors

Pin down a sheet of matboard on your drawing board. Using a draftsman's T square, lay out the walls according to the illustration. Cut them out with your heavy cutting knife. Measure the size of all openings; determine their position on the walls and rule them off with a No. 3 hard pencil. The mortar lines assist you in lining up.

Set your knife against a steel rule and cut the openings just inside the tracing lines. Take your new ½" mill file and true up the edges and corners, filing through one side and then the other. With care you can get openings just as clean as die-cut. Upon completing door and window openings set the walls aside for a minute.

Using the $\frac{3}{16}$"-square basswood, cut six corner reinforcing blocks for the mitered joints. Cut these strips slightly shorter than the walls are high. Now take your knife and bevel the ends of the walls. You can insure a perfect joint by beveling right up to the red-brick embossing. Now smooth up with your mill file. Using corner blocks already cut, cement the four walls up. After they have dried sufficiently, position and glue in the wall partition through the center of the building. The double front door is recessed back into the wall 2½ feet. The recess is cased up at the rear on the inside, the same as all other openings.

Use a scrap of $\frac{1}{16}$" scribed wood for the ceiling. Using the ⅛" x ⅛" basswood, cement a framing around the inside of the walls at the floor line. Cross-brace with the same material. Your walls should now be plumb and square. In addition, you have a ledge and joists for the flooring. Northeastern wood, size $\frac{1}{16}$" x 3", is the flooring.

Casing for Doors and Windows

Cut strips of wood $\frac{1}{32}$" x $\frac{1}{16}$" and $\frac{1}{16}$" x $\frac{1}{16}$" in lengths of about 8" to be readied for painting. For door thresholds, bevel one edge on a strip of wood, size $\frac{1}{32}$" x $\frac{3}{32}$". Add a bit of reefer orange to box car red and brush paint on three sides of wood strips. Before you begin casing up on inside of openings, mix up a bit of caboose red with white. Add a touch of Tuscan red and reduce it with thinner. Use this mixture very thin and paint (from the inside) the white edges in all openings left there when you made those cutouts.

Don't let paint run out onto the brick siding. Use a razor blade for easy-to-see cutting in casing up doors and windows, and handle your cement sparingly on this operation as you do not want any excess cement to run out and spoil the brickwork. Set the upper and lower pieces in first, then cut to size the two side pieces and set them in; they will brace and hold the upper and lower strips in. Set your casements into the walls about 2 scale inches. The back of the framing will then be about $\frac{1}{32}$" beyond the inside. Now, using $\frac{3}{32}$" wood, cement pieces around this framing to build up level for cementing in the acetate window stock. The prepainted $\frac{1}{16}$" wood is for dividers in triple and double windows. Cut correct lengths to fit snugly and cement.

Ruled Window Panes

You will need horizontally ruled lines on acetate stock for panes in casement windows. With a draftsman's ruling pen, rule off three lines spaced the correct distance apart, making the four panes. I used Pactra chocolate-brown plastic paint. This paint is fine on acetate as it sets fast and you don't get any runs with it.

Roof Construction

Construction of the two hip-type roof sections is relatively easy if you will carefully cut your material to the

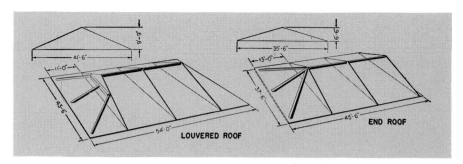

LOUVERED ROOF

END ROOF

exact size according to the illustrations. The correct pitch is absolutely necessary, otherwise it will be out of scale with the rest of the building. Referring to the illustration of louvered roof, you will note that the $\frac{1}{16}$"-thick "formers" are shown to be just under 10 scale feet high, from the bottom edge up to the peak. When you add the cardboard covering, then the sandpaper, you will build up to its required height, about 10 scale feet.

The end rafters are cut from $\frac{1}{8}$"-square basswood, and must have an angle cut on each end for fitting onto the formers and the flat sheet of $\frac{1}{16}$"-thick bottom roof section. Butt glue two 3" wide pieces of smooth basswood together for this material. The corner rafters are positioned so that an edge is at the very top. You can sight across all rafters from corner to corner and see why this one has to be turned with the edge topside.

You will also note that the rafters and formers are not set flush with the outside edges; they are cut back about $\frac{1}{8}$". The reason for setting them back is that when you fit and lay the cardboard covering on the rafters and formers their edges should feather right down to the approximate thickness of the roof base. This is achieved by beveling the underside of the cardboard where it meets the edges.

The louvers are a definite asset to the roof. Use scraps of 6" lapped siding for them. Cut two pieces of $\frac{1}{8}$"-square basswood exactly 14 scale feet long. Before cementing, position these strips on the outside in the peak of both end formers, laying them horizontally across the peaks. The top edge at the ends of these strips just touches the former edges. Make an angle cut on the strip at the ends facing the opposing roof base corner. You now have a flat surface for receiving and cementing in corner rafters. Cement two pieces of $\frac{1}{8}$"-square basswood between the formers at their points for the ridgepole.

The cardboard covering on the long sides of the roof extends 1 foot out from the peak ends, forming a triangle-shaped recess 1 foot deep back into the roof. In addition, you have a ledge for end rafters and cardboard. Cut a piece of lapped siding to fit the recess. Frame it with $\frac{1}{32}$"-square wood and cement it in back against the former. After cardboard and sandpaper are on, glue a framing of $\frac{1}{8}$"-square wood all around the underside of the roof base, positioned so that when you set it down on the tops of the walls, it will slip down on the inside, springing out the walls just enough to make them plumb. You can remove the roof at will, as you will want lighting later on. The louvered roof section extends out from the walls 4'-6" on all four sides.

Construction details for the roof of the lower half of the freight station are identical except that this roof has a lower pitch. Height and position of the formers are shown on the drawing. The roof base extends out from the walls 1'-6" on front, back and end.

Door Detail

Doors are the overhead type with panes at the top. The size of the cutouts is shown on the illustration. Work with a very sharp blade and a very thin pointed file. This $\frac{1}{32}$" plywood works beautifully, even on the tiny side lights in the double front door section. Make your cuts well inside the pencil lines; you will be surprised just how easily and perfectly you can size them up with that pointed file. All doors are cut to the exact size of the openings, and are fitted in from the back. A tiny speck of cement will hold them in. Measure the inside of the openings; cut a long strip of ply (grain vertical) the same width as the openings. Mark off and cut out each door separately, one at a time, out on the end of the strip. You have the advantage of a long piece to hang on to.

Canopies

Canopies cover the doors on the two sides of the structure. Material best suited for them is $\frac{1}{16}$"-thick plywood; it is tougher than smooth basswood and after the covering is placed on you will need to angle-drill holes through it for the rod bracing. I used No. 20 brass wire with a very small turn on one end to prevent it pulling through. These turned ends are countersunk up into the underside; the other ends are slipped into the walls of building. Use a No. 75 drill and then cement is not necessary. The sandpaper covering extends out from the edges about $\frac{1}{32}$", and additional width is left for a flash at the back side. This flash is 6" wide and you can cement it right to the sides of the building. You will note both canopies have a canter upwards. Bevel both edges, front and back; they should appear vertical when positioned against the walls. Canopies are 6'-6" wide, same as the unloading dock.

The unloading dock is a single piece of hard balsa. Risers are cut into one end. Paint and cement a strip under the three doors on the back wall for a bumper. It is advisable to use light colored paints for all woodwork and doors. Your railroad colors are fine, but you will need to lighten them up a bit with white paint. Spray-paint the roofs if possible.

BILL OF MATERIALS

2 sheets E. Suydam & Co. red brick matboard — walls
2 lengths Northeastern smooth basswood, $\frac{1}{16}$" x 3" — flooring, roofs
1 sheet $\frac{1}{32}$" plywood, 6" x 12" — doors
1 length Northeastern basswood, $\frac{3}{16}$" x $\frac{3}{16}$" — reinforcing corner blocks
2 lengths Northeastern basswood, $\frac{1}{8}$" x $\frac{1}{8}$" — inside wall bracing and floor joists
2 lengths Northeastern basswood, $\frac{1}{32}$" x $\frac{3}{32}$" — door thresholds and furring out window frames.
5 lengths Northeastern basswood, $\frac{1}{32}$" x $\frac{1}{16}$" — inside casing of door and window openings
1 length Northeastern basswood, $\frac{1}{16}$" x $\frac{1}{16}$" — dividers in triple and double windows
1 sheet No. 10 cardboard — roof
2 sheets medium fine sandpaper — roof covering
1 sheet clear acetate window stock
Coach green, boxcar red, reefer orange and concrete-colored paint
Chocolate-brown plastic paint
Ambroid or Duco cement

Branchline station

A TINY branchline station that has its prototype on the North Lake (Wis.) branch of the Milwaukee Road is a natural to build in any gauge. Your Sussex depot can be the logical heart of a tiny village. A siding or two like those shown in the photo below will serve the local industries.

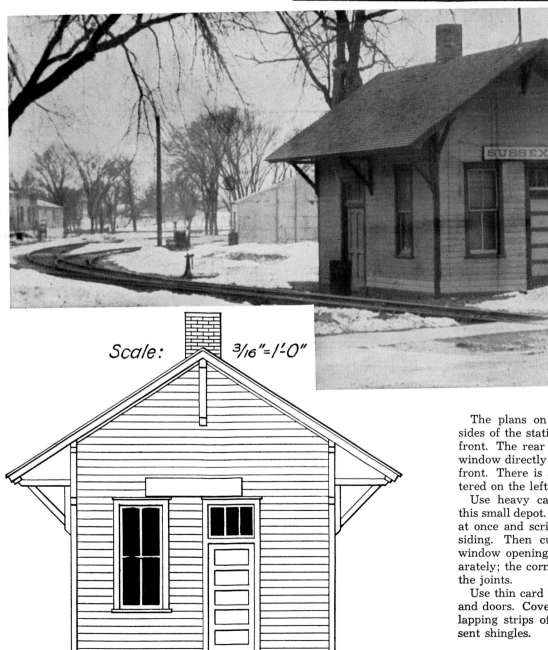

Scale: 3/16"=1'-0"

The plans on this page show two sides of the station: the right and the front. The rear side has its door and window directly opposite those on the front. There is a single window centered on the left side.

Use heavy cardboard to construct this small depot. Lay out all four sides at once and scribe them to represent siding. Then cut out the door and window openings. Cut the sides separately; the corner moldings will hide the joints.

Use thin card to frame the windows and doors. Cover the roof with overlapping strips of paper cut to represent shingles.

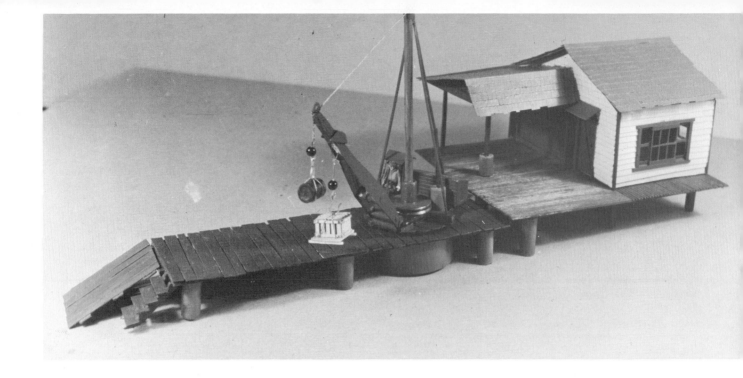

BY EUGENE LE DOUX

AN OPERATING TRACKSIDE STRUCTURE

A freight station that lowers

An operating unit for your railroad isn't as hard to build as you might think. Eugene Le Doux has this freight station on his layout; he tells you how to make one.

ONE of the first structures that most model trainmen want on their pikes is a freight station, probably because this is such a necessary building on a prototype railroad. Here's a combination freight station, platform and operating derrick that you can build yourself from materials right at hand.

There is no particular prototype for this model. You might say it is a composite of several prototypes, plus some of my own innovations. I hope you add some of your ideas, too! I think every model builder should add some-

the boom

thing original to his model, except when he is strictly following the prototype for some reason or other. In my opinion, what poetic license does for poetry, a certain amount of leeway in model building does for the completed structure.

The operating derrick and the "lit up" station are the two main features of this model, and both can be installed easily. As far as material is concerned, you could put it all together on a desert isle with nothing but an X-acto knife and a tube of glue. Seriously, though, most model trainmen will have the required materials in their scrap box. You will need: scribed wood; card stock — both heavy and thin; washers of various sizes; hollow brass tubing; ¼"-, 1⁄16"-, and 1⁄32"-square stripwood; ¼" dowel; spools — from thread; fishline or silk thread; wire and a 6-12-volt grain o' wheat bulb, yellow. Would you believe all this "junk" could be transformed into a beautiful working model? No? Then read on and see.

Let's begin with the freight station

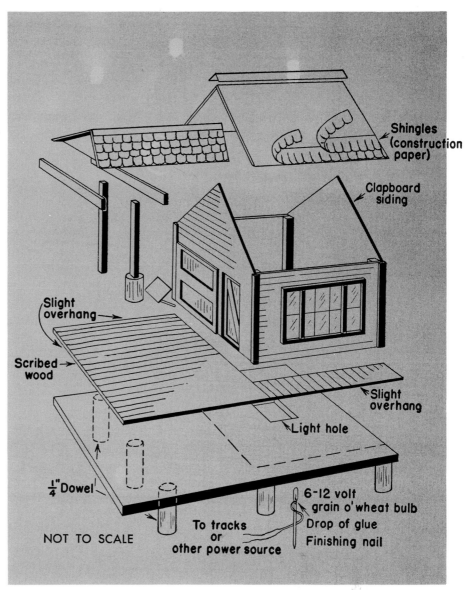

Shingles (construction paper)

Clapboard siding

Slight overhang

Scribed wood

Slight overhang

Light hole

¼" Dowel

6-12 volt grain o' wheat bulb
Drop of glue
Finishing nail

NOT TO SCALE

To tracks or other power source

Things are really moving around on this live-wire model railroad, even though one fellow is sitting down on the job. This station will look fine in a small town.

and leave the best part — the derrick — until last. Cut out the base for the station from a piece of heavy cardboard. Draw a floor plan on the base so you can tell where to glue the scribed wood flooring. Locate the center of the floor and cut a hole for the light bulb, which will be inserted later. Glue ¼"-square crossbeams to the underside of the base for added strength. Then glue the vertical posts, which support the station, to the crossbeams. Notice that the scribed-wood flooring extends over the edge of the base. This is done so that notches can be cut into the edges with a fine coping saw (or preferably a jewelers' saw) to give the floor a well-worn, individual-board appearance.

Make the clapboard siding from strips of card, one strip laid over the other. If you prefer, use commercial siding for a neater look; this also saves a lot of time. Regardless of whether you use commercial siding or not, reinforce the inside corners of

the building with pieces of ¼"- or 1⁄8"-square stripwood. Before gluing the sides together, cut out the windows and doors and add the framework, using card stock and 1⁄32"-square stripwood.

Use heavy card to make the roof and cut shingles from strips of construction paper. Finish the freight station with a coat or two of paint. I painted mine yellow, with brown trim and gray shingles.

Now you're ready to tackle the platform and operating derrick, which is really very simple. Imagine how your friends will stare in delight when they see the derrick pick up a load from a flat car, swing around and deposit it on the platform.

Cut planks from thin card stock and glue them to a heavy card base to make the floor of the platform. Make the supporting posts from ¼"-square stripwood or ¼" dowel, like those on the station. Use bits of wood and card to form the steps and gangplank,

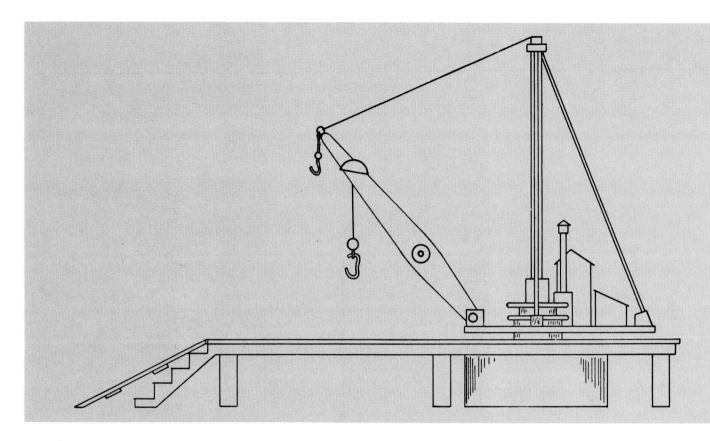

which is placed alongside the steps. The simulated concrete base below the platform rests on the ground, but the top is glued to the underside of the platform. An old Scotch-tape roll makes a perfect base for HO gauge when painted gray. Those modeling in other gauges can use a different size roll or even make one from scrap wood or cardboard.

The derrick itself consists of a deck made from heavy and thin card and then built up with washers of various sizes. To form the mast of the derrick, stick a piece of hollow brass tubing down through the center of the washers. I used 1/32"-square stripwood to brace the mast, but wire is also suitable. Before you attach the mast permanently, drill a hole in the tubing near the deck to allow a passage for the cable which raises and lowers the hook on the boom. Use pieces of scrap wood, card and wire to add details such as the control shed, controls, motor housing and pipes.

The boom for the derrick deserves special attention. Attach it to the deck of the derrick by means of the hinge-like contraption shown in the diagram, but first brace the sides of the boom with stripwood. There are two cables: one moves the boom and the other moves the hook. I suggest that you use a strong flexible material like fishline or silk thread for the cables, because they will be subject to quite a bit of friction. Both hooks are made in the same manner, but notice that

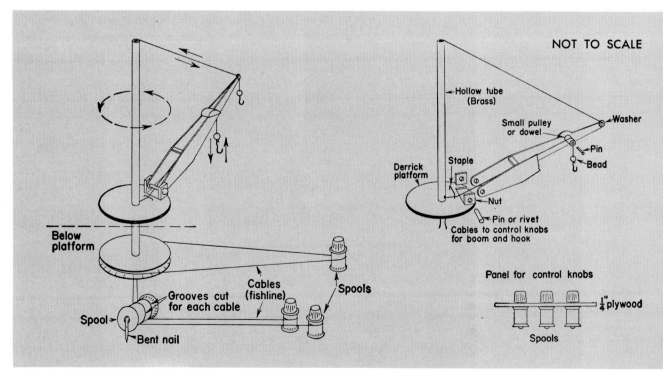

Train order stand

BY DONALD SIMS
Photos by the author

TRAIN orders play a mighty important role on most of today's railroad mileage, despite the steady inroads centralized traffic control is making. This fact proves that a method of delivering orders on your model pike would be right in line with standard operating procedure.

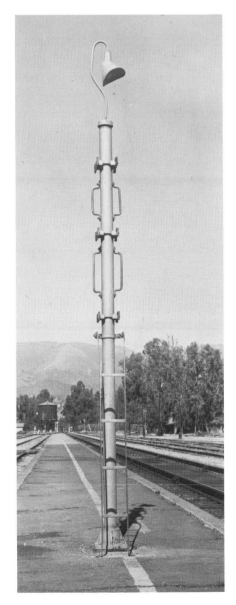

This train order stand serves a main line and a siding on the Southern Pacific Ry. Its simple construction can be duplicated on a model railroad.

One of the most common methods of getting train orders aboard a moving train is to attach them to hoops which are fastened to a fixed stand. The stand shown in the photo is in use by the Southern Pacific Ry. and serves two tracks: a main line and a siding. It has provision for three orders on each side, which means it can hold a total of six flimsies at a time. Not all fixtures for delivering up orders can hold that many, so this basic model can be altered to fit in with other situations; for instance, single-track running. Or perhaps helper engines aren't used on your pike's main line, and provision for just two orders at a time is all that is needed.

Basically the order stand is just a piece of pipe to which a ladder and a couple of grab irons have been attached. Use either wood doweling or metal tubing for the main piece. The only advantage in using the latter is that you can mount a working light at the top of the stand and run wires through it. But, other fixtures such as the ladder and receptacles for the orders may prove a little harder to mount to this tubing.

Probably the best sizes of dowel or tubing to use are ¼" for O gauge and ⅛" for HO. These are somewhat oversize but have the advantage of being a little easier to work with. The ladder which is attached to the stand can be made from a piece of freight car ladder. You'll have to bend one end in to make it fit properly. Two pairs of grab irons are required to make the hand holds. If wood is used, they can easily be pinned or glued in place.

Make the train order holders from piano wire or sections of a paper clip. Use two pieces, one slightly longer than the other. Wrap the short section around the longer one a couple of times, then shape it to a V, leaving a short segment to stick in the stand. Glue a small piece of cardboard around the joint to hide it; this will also give it a more realistic appearance.

A small piece of white plastic-sheathed wire will simulate a train order. Wrap some thread around it a few times, then repeat this operation at either end of the V-shaped holder.

Fasten it in place with a couple of drops of glue and you have a train order ready and waiting for that mainline freight.

Install this train order stand in a permanent place, or mount it on a base if you prefer to move it around the layout. Either way, it's sure to add a bit of window dressing to any station along the line.

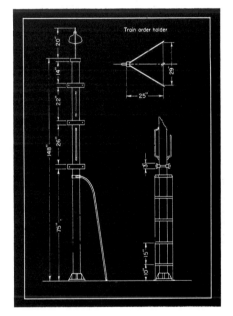

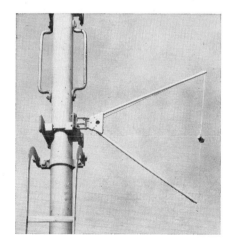

The train order hoop looks like this. It snaps easily into the bracket on the stand. A paper clip or two will make a good hoop for your flimsies.

Pick up mail on the fly

WORKING mail-pouch hangers and pouch-catcher devices can be made from scrap materials. They are simple to construct, but the sight of a train picking up the mail as it speeds past a station will add a dramatic bit of realism to your operations.

First construct the pouch hanger. Cut a piece of scale 4″ x 6″ wood 12 feet long. Make two little brackets from the same material. Glue the brackets to the post and drill a hole in the end of each bracket about a scale foot deep. Form the hanger bars from wire and glue them in the holes in the brackets.

Usually hangers are used in only one direction. If you intend to install only one at each station instead of the usual two, make the hanger bars a press fit in the bracket and don't glue them in place; then the hanger bars can be rotated 180° for opposite-direction operation. Cut and install two knee braces to give the structure more stability.

O and S gaugers can make steps from thin pieces of wood; HO gaugers

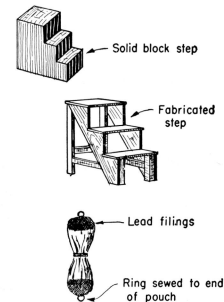

Solid block step

Fabricated step

Lead filings

Ring sewed to end of pouch

can carve them from a solid block of balsa wood.

To make the pouch catcher, cut a piece of wire about 5 scale feet long and file a point at one end. File a socket from a small piece of brass to the shape shown in the sketch. Drill a hole through it at one side and glue or solder the safety bar to the socket in the proper position. Form a catcher arm as shown in the sketch and glue or solder it in a hole drilled part way through the socket at the other side.

Slip a handrail stanchion over each end of the safety bar. Drill a hole in the postal car side on each side of the door and insert the stanchion stems. With a pair of pliers, carefully squeeze the ball on the end of the stanchion until it crimps the safety bar in place. Make it tight enough to hold the catcher arm in a horizontal or retrieving position, but loose enough to allow the arm to be moved downward to a vertical or retracted position with a little pressure. If it becomes loose after use, crimp it with pliers again.

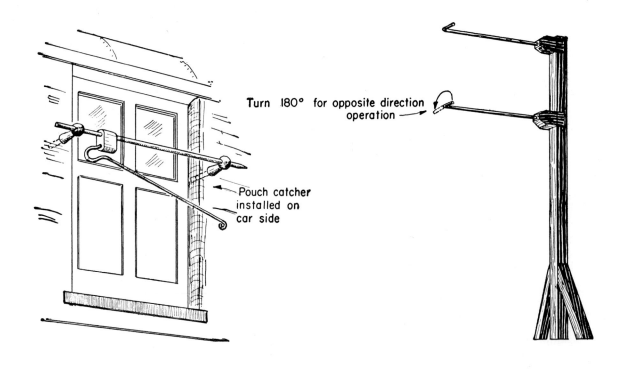

Turn 180° for opposite direction operation

Pouch catcher installed on car side

MODEL TRAINS: A. C. Kalmbach.

Here's how the mail-pouch hanger and catcher arm works on a prototype railroad, with rarely a miss! The train doesn't slow a bit, but the U. S. mail goes through because it's safely snatched up into the Railway Post Office.

The mail pouch will be easy for O gaugers to make. It is a sack, 3½ feet by 1½ feet in size, made from silk or sheer cloth. (Your wife can show you how.) Wind thread tightly around the center of the pouch; pour each end of the sack one-third full of lead filings and sew up the ends. Sew a loop of thread at the top and bottom, or form a wire loop and sew it to the bag.

HO gaugers can make a small sack using bits of solder or tiny lead shot for weight. Sew little loops of thread at the top and bottom to hook on the arms of the pouch hanger.

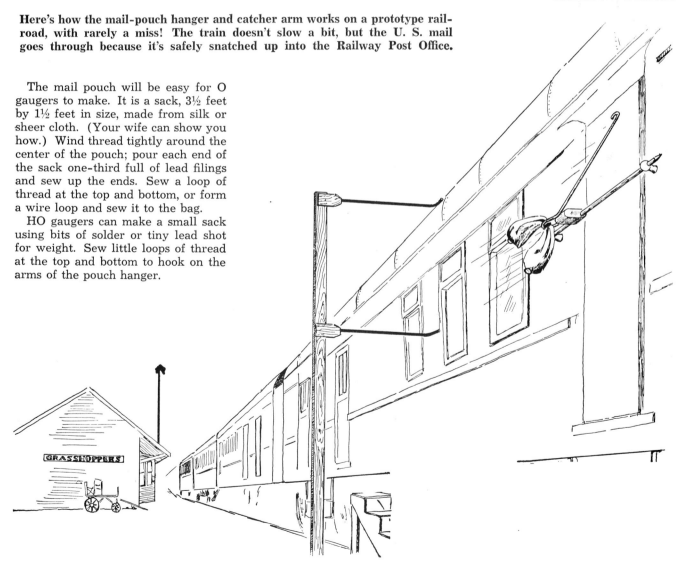

Lamps for your station platforms

Slip the wire off the dowel, bend the inserted end straight, clip the wire off to the proper length (12 feet is average lamp height), and you have a lamppost that can be duplicated as many times as you wish.

The same procedure can be used for lamps shown in Fig. 5 and Fig. 6, except that you use a block instead of a dowel as the form. The shade can be formed from bits of aluminum foil pressed to shape in a two-part wood die (Fig. 2). You can also use plastic. Most types get soft in hot water, so thin sheets of plastic could be heated until pliable, then formed in the die.

Lamp brackets shown in Figs. 7, 8 and 9 can be made from lengths of wire glued to wood dowel posts. Make ornate filigree work as shown in Fig. 3. As you cut thin strips of shim brass, they will naturally curl. You need only straighten or increase the curl slightly to get the desired effect. Glue a bead in the reflector for a bulb. Paint the post and outside of the shade black, and the inside white.

ALMOST every station has a platform lighting system. Even the small junction station has a sooty shade hung on the end of a piece of goose-necked pipe bolted to the wall. The most common lamp types are shown here and the method described tells how to make a number of posts and shades, all the same size.

If you make the type shown in Fig. 4, get a small piece of dowel the same diameter as the curve of the post. Two scale feet is about right. Drill a small hole in one side, insert an end of a piece of soft brass wire and bend it around the dowel (Fig. 1). The wire should be about a scale 3″ in diameter.

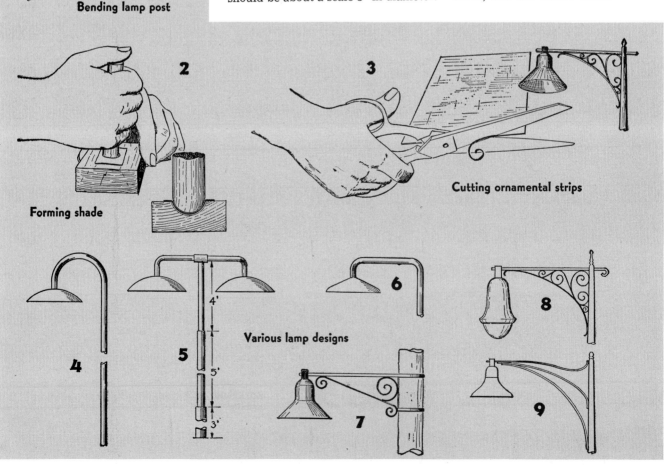

Bending lamp post

Forming shade

Cutting ornamental strips

Various lamp designs

Build this platform shed

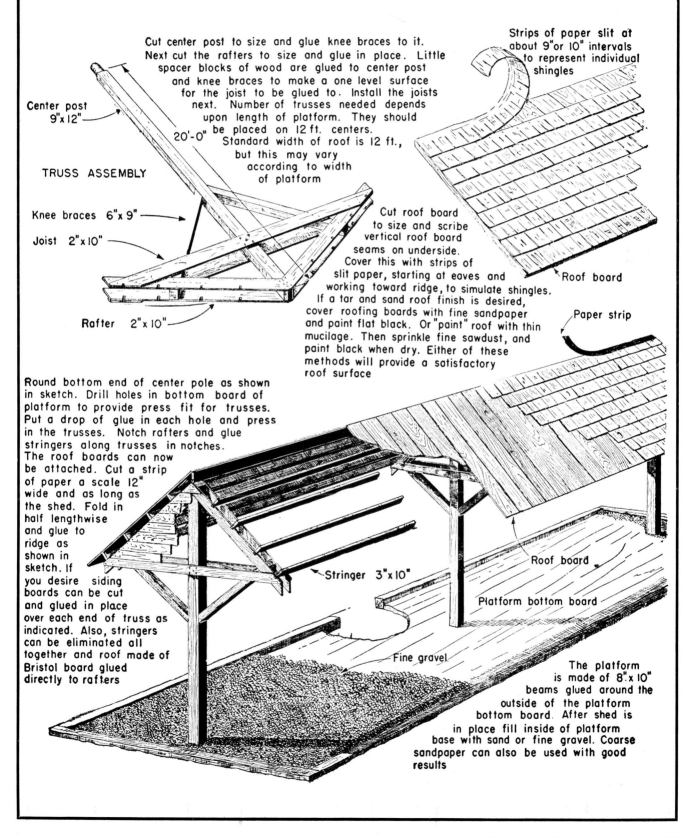

Cut center post to size and glue knee braces to it. Next cut the rafters to size and glue in place. Little spacer blocks of wood are glued to center post and knee braces to make a one level surface for the joist to be glued to. Install the joists next. Number of trusses needed depends upon length of platform. They should be placed on 12 ft. centers. Standard width of roof is 12 ft., but this may vary according to width of platform

Center post 9"x12"

20'-0"

TRUSS ASSEMBLY

Knee braces 6"x 9"

Joist 2"x 10"

Rafter 2"x 10"

Strips of paper slit at about 9"or 10" intervals to represent individual shingles

Cut roof board to size and scribe vertical roof board seams on underside. Cover this with strips of slit paper, starting at eaves and working toward ridge, to simulate shingles. If a tar and sand roof finish is desired, cover roofing boards with fine sandpaper and paint flat black. Or "paint" roof with thin mucilage. Then sprinkle fine sawdust, and paint black when dry. Either of these methods will provide a satisfactory roof surface

Roof board

Paper strip

Round bottom end of center pole as shown in sketch. Drill holes in bottom board of platform to provide press fit for trusses. Put a drop of glue in each hole and press in the trusses. Notch rafters and glue stringers along trusses in notches. The roof boards can now be attached. Cut a strip of paper a scale 12" wide and as long as the shed. Fold in half lengthwise and glue to ridge as shown in sketch. If you desire siding boards can be cut and glued in place over each end of truss as indicated. Also, stringers can be eliminated all together and roof made of Bristol board glued directly to rafters

Stringer 3"x 10"

Roof board

Platform bottom board

Fine gravel

The platform is made of 8".x 10" beams glued around the outside of the platform bottom board. After shed is in place fill inside of platform base with sand or fine gravel. Coarse sandpaper can also be used with good results

The platform is made of wood, but the grainy finish given by the author makes it look like the concrete prototype.

A concrete loading platform

BY ROBERT E. GILBERT

Photos by the author

THE concrete loading platform near the Southern Railway station in Jonesboro, Tenn., makes a simple but attractive model. If you have not yet attempted to build a structure from scratch, try out your skill on this easy platform.

As you can see when you examine the plans, there are only two parts. You whittle the bulk of the platform from a block of wood, and then cement a 3" x 6" timber to the back edge. The dimensions given are not necessarily critical, and you may vary them slightly.

For ease in carving, I used balsa wood, but other woods are suitable. If you do not have a single block of the correct thickness, cement thinner pieces together to make one.

Cut the block to a scale 4 x 16 x 37 feet. Keep sides and corners square.

On top of the block, measure back 16 feet from the front and draw a line. At the back of the block, draw a line 6" up from the bottom. On each side, connect the ends of these lines to mark the slope of the ramp.

Use a sharp knife to whittle away the wood until you are working close to the guide lines. Give the ramp a final level surface with a sanding block, which you can make by wrapping a sheet of sandpaper around a piece of wood. Paint the platform with about two coats of sanding sealer, to hide the grain of the wood; then sand it lightly.

Details not often found on models of concrete structures are the impressions left by the wooden form into which the concrete is poured. If you want to indicate these, take a small screwdriver with a blade 8 or 9 scale inches wide. Use a ruler as a guide and run the flat of the blade along the front and sides of the model. Then move down slightly more than the width of the screwdriver and repeat. This procedure leaves narrow ridges in the wood.

To imitate the rough, grainy texture of the prototype, sift sand through cloth and mix the resulting dust with light gray model railroad

Cracks scribed into the completed model add realism to the loading platform.

paint. Brush one or two coats of this mixture on the model, but do not paint the back edge.

After the paint has dried, scribe a few cracks along the ridge on the front and sides.

For the second part of the model, cut a timber 3″ x 6″ x 16′-0″. Cement it to the back edge of the platform.

Add water stains and dirt to the platform with thin washes of brown and yellowish paint, or by brushing on powdered chalk or pastels.

On your layout, locate the front of the model 6′-6″ from the center line of a siding. If you do not have room for this installation, you may place it with the sides parallel to the track. Fill in around the platform with cinders or gravel, making sure that the fill comes to the top of the timber.

The prototype platform stands near the Southern Railway station at Jonesboro, Tenn. Note the impressions left from wooden forms, and the dirt on top.

CONCRETE LOADING PLATFORM — HO SCALE

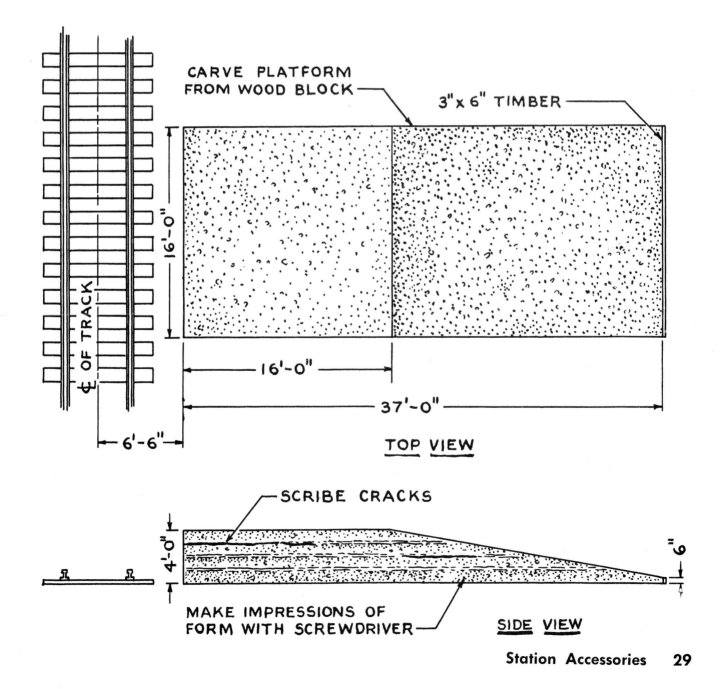

CARVE PLATFORM FROM WOOD BLOCK

3″ x 6″ TIMBER

℄ OF TRACK

16′-0″

16′-0″

37′-0″

6′-6″

TOP VIEW

SCRIBE CRACKS

4′-0″

6″

MAKE IMPRESSIONS OF FORM WITH SCREWDRIVER

SIDE VIEW

End-loading ramp

FOR YOUR PIGGYBACK SERVICE

BY ROBERT E. GILBERT

All illustrations by the author

AFTER you build an end-loading ramp at the end of a siding or yard track, your railroad will move freight in several new ways. In the combined trucking and railroading operation known as piggyback freight, a tractor-trailer truck can back up the ramp onto a flat car, where the trailer will be unhitched and secured for transportation by rail. Other flat-car loads, such as farm machinery and bulldozers, may be handled with an end-loading ramp, and if you have drop-end gondolas or special lumber or automobile box cars with end doors, the ramp will be useful for them.

The prototype for the model ramp stands behind the Norfolk & Western Ry. and Southern Ry. freight station in Bristol, Va. By building with wood strips, you can duplicate the heavy timbers of the full-size structure.

Before you begin construction, notice one difference between prototype and model couplers. Since most model automatic couplers have an uncoupling pin hanging close to the track, the pin will hit the bumper in front of the ramp when you back a car into position. This slight problem can be solved either by omitting the bumper or making it movable. If you

want the pin of an automatic coupler to fit the opening in the front of the ramp, cut a slot through the two top members of the front pier.

Perhaps you have enough wood strips on hand to build the ramp; if not, you can cut some pieces to acquire all the sizes. Northeastern Scale Models is one source of the necessary strips. In the list of materials, the full-size timbers approximated in an HO model are also given. You can use these full-size figures to select wood in other scales. Stripwood dimensions mentioned in the following text are for HO.

Top

Study the plans and cut four 24'-6" stringers from $\frac{3}{32}$" x $\frac{3}{16}$" wood. Cement the edges of the strips together to form two pairs. With a drop or two of cement, lightly tack the strips to your work surface or a piece of cardboard, spacing the outer edges of the pairs 9'-6" apart.

For the top timbers, cut 26 pieces of $\frac{1}{8}$"-square wood 10'-0" long and two pieces 3'-3" long. In all but the two timbers at the back of the ramp, cut two notches $1\frac{1}{2}$" deep on one edge of each timber as shown on the plan. The notches form a tread for truck wheels.

Attach the cross timbers to the stringers, letting them extend 3" at either side. When the cement has dried, detach the stringers from your work surface. At the front of the top, measure down 3" and back 2'-3". Whittle and sand an even slope to these lines.

Sides

The two sides will later be connected by the piers and covered by the top. To make a side, cement three 24'-6" lengths of $\frac{1}{16}$" x $\frac{3}{16}$" material together at the edges. On the center strip, you will add seven $\frac{3}{32}$" x $\frac{3}{16}$" parts in two layers. Look at the side view in the plan and locate the bottom layer. Measure $\frac{5}{32}$" from the front and attach the 5'-0" section. Measure $\frac{1}{8}$" from the end of it and add the 4'-0" part. The 10'-0" section toward the back should have the last 3'-0" of its length sloped to a 3" thickness at the end.

The second layer has, at the front, an upright with the top slanted $1\frac{1}{2}$". This part should be about $25\frac{1}{2}$" long to make the height of the side 3'-3". Behind the upright, place a diagonal brace as shown in the drawing. Add the other two pieces to complete the side.

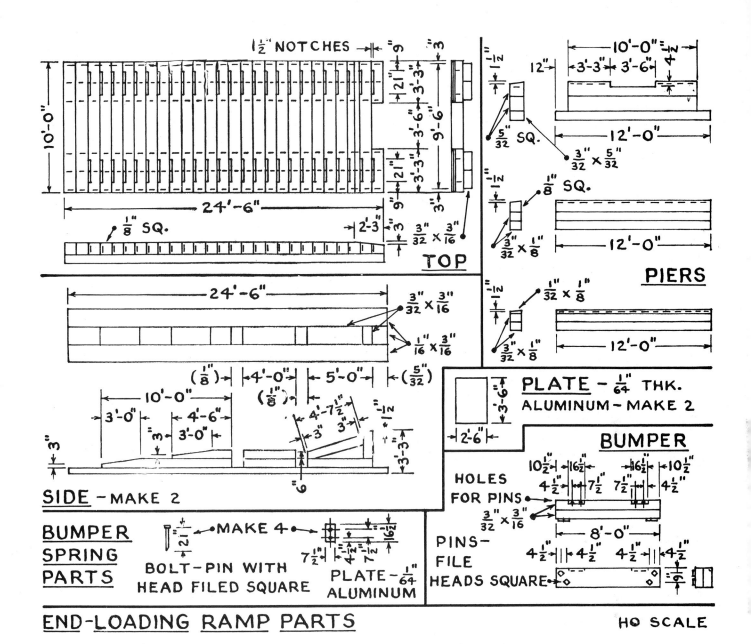

TOP

PIERS

PLATE – $\frac{1}{64}$" THK.
ALUMINUM – MAKE 2

SIDE – MAKE 2

BUMPER

BUMPER SPRING PARTS

MAKE 4

BOLT-PIN WITH HEAD FILED SQUARE

PLATE – $\frac{1}{64}$" ALUMINUM

HOLES FOR PINS

PINS – FILE HEADS SQUARE

END-LOADING RAMP PARTS

HO SCALE

The prototype ramp in Bristol, Va., is shown below, just waiting to be scaled down for your road. Parts are above.

The front view of the author's end-loading ramp. That loafer will probably jump when a flat car bumps against the ramp and a truck backs up onto it.

Piers

The front pier has two 5/32″-square strips 10′-0″ long resting on a 3/32″ x 5/32″ strip 12′-0″ long. Slant the top piece 1½″ and cut a 4½″ x 3′-6″ notch in the center of it. Make the two back piers from 12′-0″ pieces as detailed on the plan.

Plates

You need two metal plates, about 2′-6″ x 3′-6″, to bridge the gap between ramp and flat car when loading. Aluminum 1/64″ thick is suitable for these and is easier to cut and file than brass or tin.

Ramp assembly

Space the two sides 12′-0″ apart from outer edge to outer edge. Cement the front pier in position on the bottom strips and against the upright

braces. Place the other two piers in their slots. Check the slanting surfaces by holding a ruler across them to be sure that all the slopes are in line. Cement the top to the sides and piers.

Paint the ramp a dark brown to simulate creosote. The metal plates may be laid on the platform or fastened with cement.

Bumper

If you want to build the bumper, cement two 8′-0″ timbers, 3/32″ x 3/16″,

together. In the back timber, cut notches 16½″ wide, with the bottom of the notches slanting about 40 degrees, to receive the spring plates.

Make four bolts for the front timber from small pins. Hold the pins in a pair of pliers and file the heads square. Cut the pins about 1/32″ below the heads, punch holes in the timber, and cement the pins in the holes.

To simulate the rods and springs holding the prototype bumper to the rails, make four 7½″ x 16½″ plates on 1/64″-thick aluminum. Punch two holes in each plate and cut the parts from the sheet. File the heads of four pins square and cut the pins about 21″ below the heads. With four springs about 3/64″ x 1/8″ — such as draft-gear springs — at hand, assemble the units by pushing two pins through a plate, slipping on the springs, and adding another plate.

Stick the spring assemblies into the back timber, so that they slant upward at a 50-degree angle. Paint the bumper to match the ramp.

Installation

When you put your completed end-loading ramp on your layout, the front should be almost against the ends of the rails. The top of the prototype is 3′-9″ above the top of the rails, and this model will scale to about that height for most kinds of HO track. Since flat-car heights may be anything from 3′-0″ on up, slight differences will not matter.

Whittle a wood block for the slope at the back of the ramp, and cover it with model dirt and gravel or cinders. The lower timbers of the prototype are also covered at the sides.

Place the bumper about 15″ from the front of the ramp, and your line is ready for new business.

Even in scale size, the timbers which form the platform of the ramp look large. Note the notches in the timbers; these form a tread for the wheels.

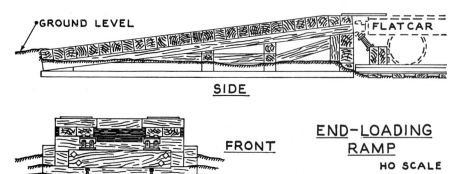

GROUND LEVEL

FLATCAR

SIDE

FRONT

END-LOADING RAMP

HO SCALE

Open-air engine shed

BY
C. F. WILEY

SCALE IN FEET

0 2 4 6 8 10   15

PERHAPS you've driven the last spike in your mainline track, and you'd like to settle down to the serious business of creating atmosphere on your layout by putting up structures and scenery. Whether you choose to model the mountains of the Pacific Northwest or the cornfields of Iowa may have a lot to do with the type of structures you'll plan to put along your right of way. For instance, if you're planning a railroad that will run through the sunny South, here's an enginehouse that's easy to build and yet true to prototype.

Down in Florida, where the weather is usually congenial, there is a short line whose single hog has an open-air enginehouse that is unusual enough to be unique. You don't necessarily have to turn your railroad into a banana route, but if you have a little feeder line you might want to model this structure instead of planning a complicated, too-large roundhouse.

Essentially this enginehouse is nothing more than a galvanized metal gable roof supported by columns and built over a short length of siding. The size of your locomotive will have a lot to do with determining the number of bays and the length of the structure, but in any case place the concrete footings so that the columns and the roof will afford a comfortable, dry and shady retreat for the engine when it is standing in the house. The width will

Easy-to-Build Model Railroad Structures

PART 3: TERMINAL AND YARD FACILITIES

depend on existing tolerances; just be sure to get the engine under cover.

Each pair of columns with the adjoining roof members forms an integral unit of a simple truss system.

Construct as many of these as you need with the aid of a jig to insure uniformity. Scale your lumber to get 10″ x 10″ or 12″ x 12″ columns, and carry out the rest of the pattern in 2 x 4's. Note that every column has diagonal braces to the cross horizontal member and also to the horizontal top plate running along under the eaves.

Look for corrugated cardboard or an old rubber stair tread; with luck you may find some just the right size for your gauge. Cut a piece to fit the roof of your enginehouse and glue it in place. Then give the roof a coat of aluminum paint so it will look like metal. For an aged, rusty look, brush on a thin coat of burnt sienna mixed with turps and wipe it nearly off with a cloth. Creosote your lumber, for in southern climates termites are destructive pests.

A TWO-STALL ENGINEHOUSE

A pike without a turntable can still protect its engines with this two-stall building; a handy table of dimensions makes it adaptable to HO, S and O gauge layouts

BY EUGENE LE DOUX

IF YOU have any engines at all, you'll need an enginehouse to protect them from the weather and to use as a shop when making minor repairs. I've chosen to model the rectangular two-stall enginehouse for various reasons. First of all, this type needs no extra paraphernalia installed along with it. A roundhouse, on the other hand, requires a turntable. Many of us cannot or do not want to install a turntable on our layouts. If this is true in your case, then this enginehouse is what you're looking for. It takes up a space 5½2" wide by 12" long in HO scale, which is fine for medium-size locos; it may have to be made longer for larger ones.

Before I go any farther, let me say one thing. Perhaps you have already noticed that this enginehouse is similar to the one built by John Allen. It's true, the inspiration to build this model did come from John Allen's exquisite masterpiece. Can you blame me? If you have seen it, you know what I mean. However, it is not a duplicate as you can see. A large railroad concern must use the same plan many times to build structures along its line. The prototype which we claim to follow never loses any sleep over duplication, so why should we? With that matter taken care of, let's go on.

This model is fairly simple and not

Your finished enginehouse should look like this model. Strips of gray construction paper simulate slate shingles.

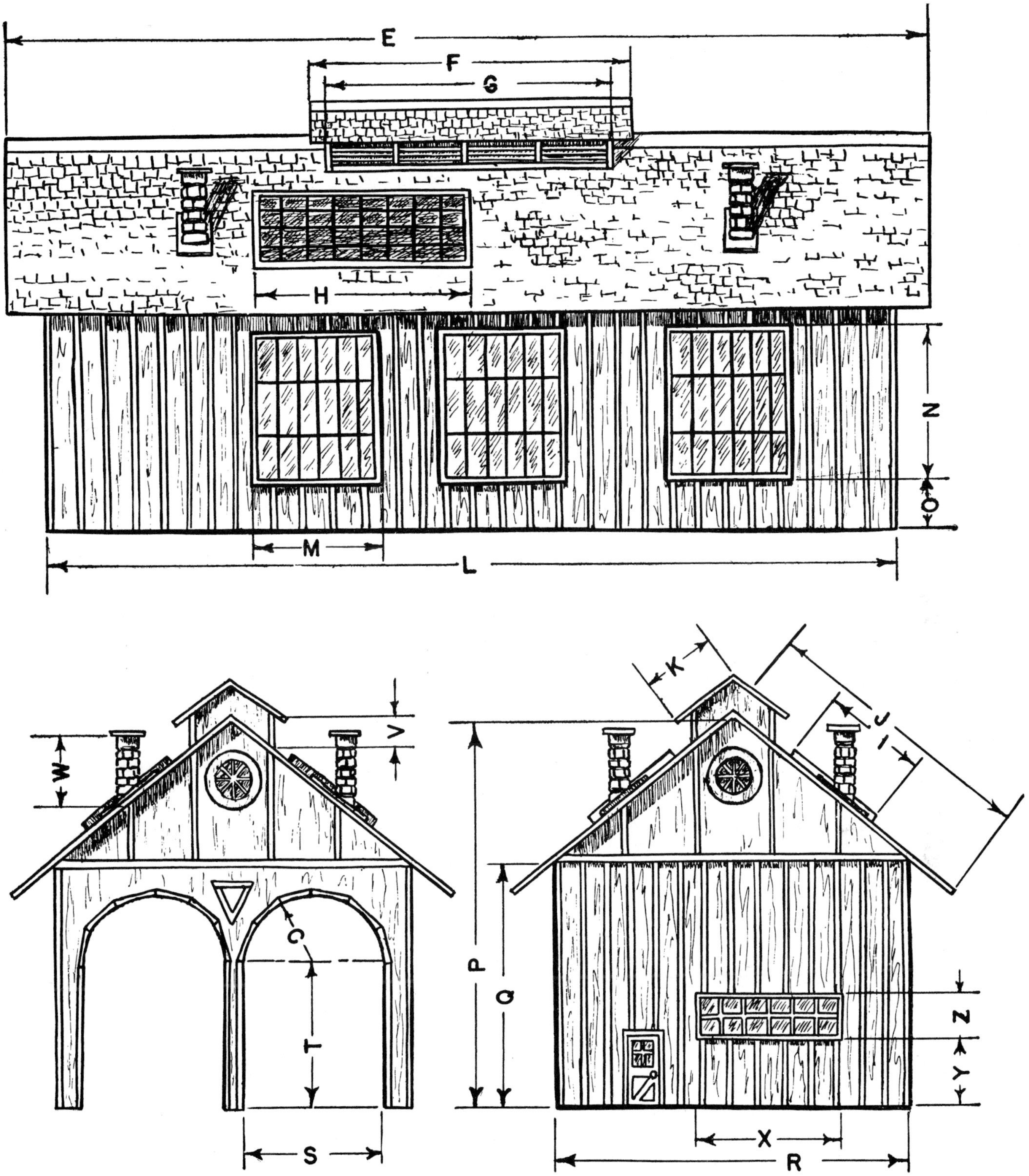

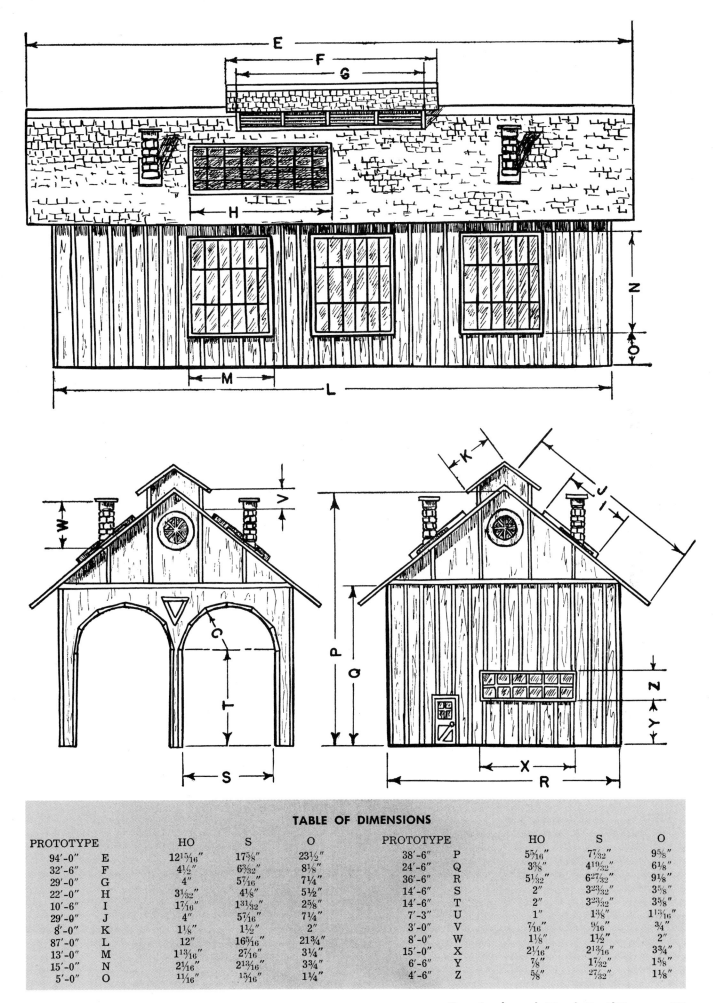

TABLE OF DIMENSIONS

PROTOTYPE		HO	S	O	PROTOTYPE		HO	S	O
94′-0″	E	12 15/16″	17 5/8″	23 1/2″	38′-6″	P	5 5/16″	7 7/32″	9 5/8″
32′-6″	F	4 1/2″	6 3/32″	8 1/8″	24′-6″	Q	3 3/8″	4 19/32″	6 1/8″
29′-0″	G	4″	5 7/16″	7 1/4″	36′-6″	R	5 1/32″	6 27/32″	9 1/8″
22′-0″	H	3 1/32″	4 1/8″	5 1/2″	14′-6″	S	2″	3 23/32″	3 5/8″
10′-6″	I	1 7/16″	1 31/32″	2 5/8″	14′-6″	T	2″	3 23/32″	3 5/8″
29′-0″	J	4″	5 7/16″	7 1/4″	7′-3″	U	1″	1 3/8″	1 13/16″
8′-0″	K	1 1/8″	1 1/2″	2″	3′-0″	V	7/16″	9/16″	3/4″
87′-0″	L	12″	16 5/16″	21 3/4″	8′-0″	W	1 1/8″	1 1/2″	2″
13′-0″	M	1 13/16″	2 7/16″	3 1/4″	15′-0″	X	2 1/16″	2 13/16″	3 3/4″
15′-0″	N	2 1/16″	2 13/16″	3 3/4″	6′-6″	Y	7/8″	1 7/32″	1 5/8″
5′-0″	O	11/16″	15/16″	1 1/4″	4′-6″	Z	5/8″	27/32″	1 1/8″

too much material is required. The sizes of stripwood you will need for any scale are in the table below. Miscellaneous material required is: construction board or quality cardboard; Northeastern capped siding (optional); celluloid; gray construction paper; paper masking tape (optional).

Here is the construction procedure I used. The sides and ends were completed and then glued together; the roof was added last. I'll take the sections in that order. All dimensions in the text are for HO scale; if you're building to another scale, use the table of dimensions for easy conversion.

Sides

Both sides are made the same way, but one is the reverse of the other as shown in the side view of the plans. Each side is 12" long by 3⅜" high. The batten or capped siding may either be purchased from your hobby dealer or it can be homemade, using cardboard and 1/32" square stripwood. Northeastern makes capped siding in wood sheets that looks very realistic. If you decide to make your own, space the 1/32" square strips approximately ⅛" apart. Brace the inside of the cardboard with ⅛" square stripwood after you have cut out the windows. See plans for correct spacing.

Don't forget to reverse the plans when making the opposite side. All window frame material is 1/16" square. There are two ways to make the window sash. One way is to use 1/32" square strips. The other method uses narrow strips of Scotch masking tape fastened directly to the celluloid window material. You can get a slight 3-D appearance by shadowing (1) half of one side on each vertical strip and (2) the lower half on each horizontal strip. (See insert on plans.) After the sides are painted, celluloid windows can be glued to the inside. Put these two pieces aside temporarily until the ends are completed.

Ends

Both ends of the enginehouse can be cut at once. They measure 5 1/32" wide, 3⅜" high to the lowest point of the roof slant, and 5 5/16" high in the center to the peak. In the front end each entrance is 2" wide and 3" high at the highest point. This should be enough clearance for any locomotive.

Frame the entire front end with 1/16" square stripwood as shown on the plans. Brace both ends with ⅛" square wood glued to the inside of the walls. I omitted doors for the sake of simplicity and convenience, but you may add them to your model if you wish.

The circular window near the peak in each end is ½" in diameter for HO gauge. (S gauge, 21/32"; O gauge, ⅞".) The crosspieces for this window can be made with 1/32" square stripwood or tape, or strips of construction paper. The rear, unlike the front of the enginehouse, is made of batten or capped siding, whatever you prefer to call it. Notice that the siding does not continue all the way to the roof but stops at a crosspiece 3⅜" up the wall. The upper half is like the front.

The doorway in the back for "human engines" is made by using bits of card stock with the usual pinhead for a doorknob. Framework for the doorway and window is 1/16" square wood. The sash for this window should be made the same way in which the ones on the side were. Paint the ends and apply celluloid for windows where needed. When assembling ends and sides, make sure that all corners are square. Hold them in position with common pins until the glue dries if it is necessary. Then make the roof.

Roof

The roof is made from one large piece of cardboard 8" wide by 12 15/16" long. Scribe this piece directly down the center and then bend it. Cut out a space for the skylights on each side. The chimneys are made of ¼" square balsa, which makes it easier to carve bricks in the sides. Make a hole down through the top using about a No. 26 drill. The skylight is made the same as the other windows.

Slate shingles were used to lessen the possibility of fire due to a spark from a smokestack. They can be made in either of two ways, the only main difference being the material used. Slate can be simulated by cutting ¼" wide strips of gray construction paper. Cut slits at intervals of approximately 1/16" in this strip. You could also use Scotch paper tape in the same way and save yourself a job of gluing.

The final addition to the roof is the cupola. Cut out two 4" x 7/16" pieces of card. These are the sides of the cupola. Glue them to an inverted V-shaped piece of card. Make sure the angle of the V is the same as the slant of the roof. After these are glued, placed 1/16" square framework where shown in the plans; 1/16" x 1/32" stripwood is used for the ventilating strips between vertical posts 1" apart on the cupola sides. Put a roof 4½" x 2¼" on the cupola and glue it to the enginehouse roof. If there should be any gaps between the bottom edge of the cupola and the enginehouse roof, fill in that space with plastic wood and smooth it out with your finger while it is still wet. Paint and weather your model when the assembly is finished.

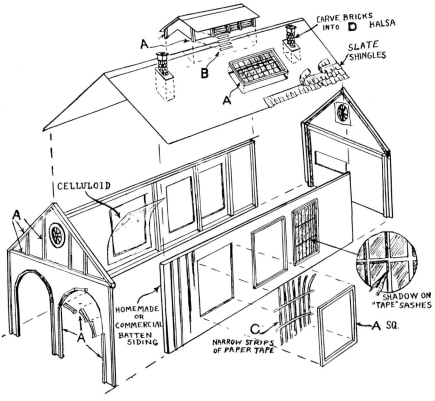

CARVE BRICKS INTO **D** BALSA

SLATE SHINGLES

CELLULOID

SHADOW ON "TAPE" SASHES

HOMEMADE OR COMMERCIAL BATTEN SIDING

NARROW STRIPS OF PAPER TAPE

A SQ.

BILL OF MATERIALS FOR STRIPWOOD

	HO	S	O
A	1/16" x 1/16"	3/32" x 3/32"	⅛" x ⅛"
B	1/16" x 1/32"	3/32" x 1/16"	⅛" x 1/16"
C	1/32" x 1/32"	1/16" x 1/16"	1/16" x 1/16"
D	¼" x ¼"	⅜" x ⅜"	½" x ½"

NOTE: Bracing on inside of walls should be ⅛" square for HO, 3/16" square for S, ¼" square for O gauge.

PROVIDE ACTIVITY AT THE DEPOT WITH . . .

Car service pits

A CAR service pit is simply a shallow enclosed hole in the ground with connections for water, steam, oil, lubrication and electrical servicing. Hinged covers open from either side. The pit is about 18″ deep, 2 feet wide and 4 feet long. It contains a maze of pipes, fittings, cables, switches, valves and sockets. Service pits are usually found in passenger car yards and along main lines at depots. They are placed about 150 feet apart, painted red, yellow or gray.

Many HO gaugers will not care to model the pit interior, for its parts in 3.5 mm. scale would be quite small. They can, however, make the cover as shown in the first sketch by scribing the cover outline on a thin piece of wood or file card and adding wire handles.

O gauge modelers can more easily fabricate the pit interior. The pit shell can be a piece of file card bent to the desired shape and the ends cemented together. Pipes can be short lengths of wire pushed through holes in the shell and cemented in place. The valves can be blobs of cement on the wire, with infant-size dress snaps for valve handles. Cement the cover frame to the top edge of the pit shell. Push a short length of wire through loops on the ends of the two thin metal cover pieces and into brackets on the cover frame to provide a working hinge. Make the hoses and cables from soft copper wire. Curve them in a natural limp fashion and paint them dull black. You could also use heavy black thread for this.

To create interest, model a scene such as the one shown at the top of the page. Place a car at the service pit and some men at the car, each performing an operation.

Terminal and Yard Facilities   37

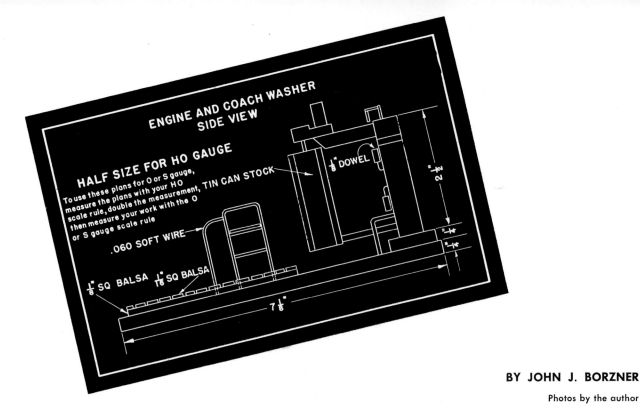

ENGINE AND COACH WASHER
SIDE VIEW

HALF SIZE FOR HO GAUGE
To use these plans for O or S gauge,
measure the plans with your HO
scale rule, double the measurement,
then measure your work with the O
or S gauge scale rule

4/8" DOWEL

TIN CAN STOCK

.060 SOFT WIRE

1/8" SQ BALSA   1/16" SQ BALSA

7 1/8"

BY JOHN J. BORZNER

Photos by the author

KEEP IT CLEAN!

Wash your rolling stock

DID YOU ever wonder who keeps the stainless steel coach bodies and the colorfully painted diesel engines gleaming? Or who washes the multitude of windows on the average streamliner? Workers do, of course, but not without the bull work being done first by the rugged engine and coach washers used by many railroads.

These washers work on same principle as the now common minute washes for automobiles. The engine which is to be cleaned travels at a snail's pace through the machine, usually hauling several cars for laundering also. As each unit enters, it is deluged with gallons of water on the top and sides. Then, as it moves forward, huge revolving brushes swing in and brush it; more water rinses away the dirt. Immediately after it leaves the brushes, it is met by wipers who chamois the windows and trim. The result is as spic and span a streamliner as ever hit the road.

I spotted the particular rack I wanted to model at the huge East Syracuse (N. Y.) yards of the New York Central. It was well hidden from public view, though probably not intentionally. This fact caused me much inconvenience. First I had to get permission to hike down onto the tracks where this machine was located. Then after I managed to take just one picture of an engine coming at me through the washer, I was thoroughly saturated.

The soaking made me abandon all attempts to secure accurate measurements of the real equipment, but the

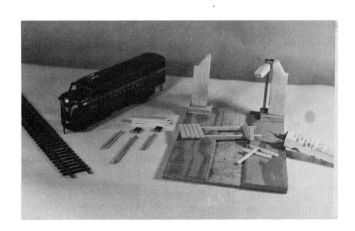

1 Begin building the washer by cutting out all parts; apply two coats of sanding sealer to each piece.

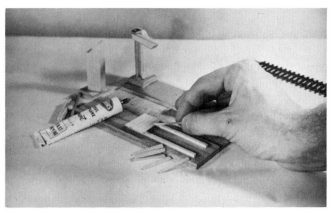

2 Cement 1/16"-thick balsa strips to two 1/8"-square runners to make walkways for the engine washer.

Engine washers for railroads operate on the same principle as minute auto washes; workers add the finishing touches.

dimensions I give in this article were carefully derived from observations and from the picture. All of this means that if you want to scale up the plans to a different gauge, remember the basic proportions. The base is approximately the length of a diesel A unit. The brush height equals the height of the sides of the engine and cars, and the overhead spray nozzles are about one foot above the air horns. Minor variations in dimensions won't be noticeable if you keep these basic proportions in mind.

The base on the prototype washer is a poured concrete platform upon which the rack is built. On my model, which is HO gauge, I used a 5" x 7⅛" piece of ¼" plywood. Cut a channel in the base about ⅛" deep and wide enough to accommodate your track.

The walks can be made from balsa wood. Cut a 1/16" sheet of balsa into several strips 1¼" long by about ¼" wide. Next, glue these strips to two ⅛"-square runners. You need two walks 3¾" long.

The scaffolds used by the window

wipers are made from soft wire of about .060" thickness. Egg-crate binding works very well for this. Make four sides as shown in the side view. Drill holes in a piece of scrap pine at the six points designated by circles in the top view. This is a temporary base for the scaffold frames during soldering. Stand the sides upright in the holes and solder in the cross pieces. Note carefully how the ladder is attached to the main rack. A piece of 1/16" sheet balsa can be used for the flooring of the scaffolds.

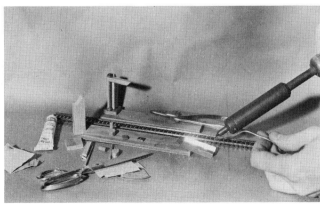

3 Solder seams in the corners of the splash pans, and also solder a small nail through the holes indicated.

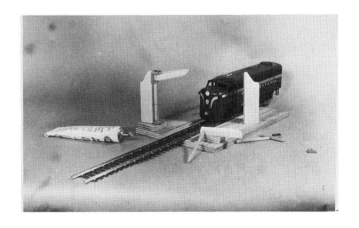

4 Make subassemblies of the support arms and dowels before attaching them; dowels move freely in place.

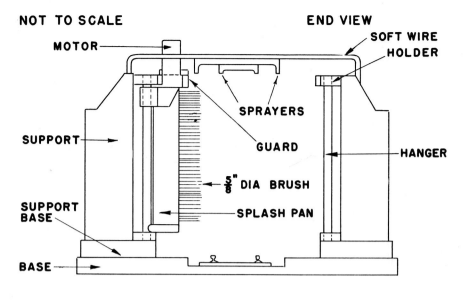

NOT TO SCALE

MOTOR

SUPPORT

SUPPORT BASE

BASE

END VIEW

SOFT WIRE HOLDER

SPRAYERS

GUARD

$\frac{5}{8}$" DIA BRUSH

SPLASH PAN

HANGER

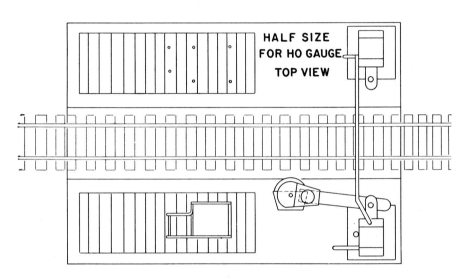

HALF SIZE FOR HO GAUGE TOP VIEW

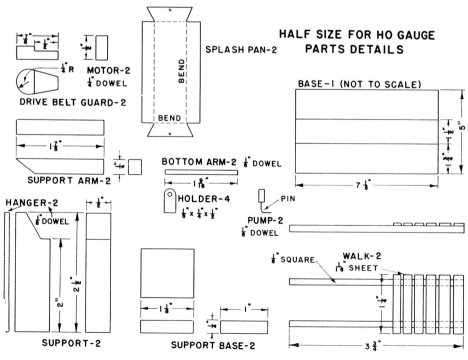

HALF SIZE FOR HO GAUGE PARTS DETAILS

MOTOR-2 $\frac{1}{4}$" DOWEL

DRIVE BELT GUARD-2 $\frac{1}{4}$" R

SPLASH PAN-2 BEND BEND

BASE-1 (NOT TO SCALE) 5" 7$\frac{1}{4}$"

SUPPORT ARM-2 1$\frac{7}{8}$"

BOTTOM ARM-2 $\frac{1}{8}$" DOWEL 1$\frac{3}{8}$"

HOLDER-4 $\frac{1}{8}$" x $\frac{1}{4}$" x $\frac{1}{2}$"

PIN

PUMP-2 $\frac{1}{4}$" DOWEL

HANGER-2 $\frac{1}{8}$" DOWEL 2$\frac{1}{4}$" 2"

SUPPORT-2

$\frac{1}{8}$" SQUARE

WALK-2 $\frac{1}{16}$" SHEET 3$\frac{3}{4}$"

SUPPORT BASE-2 1$\frac{1}{8}$" 1"

Wipe away all the flux from the joints and paint the scaffolds and walks flat black. Drill the six holes in the position shown into the walkways, and insert the scaffolds permanently in these holes, which are about $\frac{1}{8}$" deep. Set these assemblies aside for attaching to the rack later.

Make the two upright supports for the brushes from hardwood, which takes paint better and is stronger than balsa. Cut each support to the dimension shown so it will fit well; sand the supports smooth and apply one or two coats of sanding sealer. Light sanding after sealing will prepare the parts for painting.

To assemble the washer, glue the support bases, $\frac{1}{4}$" x 1" x 1$\frac{1}{8}$", to the washer base. Next add the main upright supports. Attach the small hydraulic cylinders to the one upright.

Slip the support arm down a $\frac{1}{8}$" x 2$\frac{1}{2}$" dowel and attach it to the two $\frac{1}{4}$" x $\frac{1}{2}$" swivel holders. The brush drive belt guard and motors are glued to the end of the support arms as in the top view. Then these assemblies are attached to the main upright supports. Paint the entire assembly a light gray, and the motors black.

Make the splash pans from tin can stock, cut to the pattern shown. Solder the top and bottom edges to the sides, and also solder a small nail to the top edge through the hole indicated. As for brushes, any type can be used that has a diameter of $\frac{5}{8}$". I used a coffeemaker's glass neck brush, cut to the size needed and soldered through the bottom hole in each pan. Paint the pans gray, but be careful not to get paint on the brushes.

Attach the pans to the supports by pushing the nail in the top through the drive belt guard. Be sure the pans are vertical.

Glue the walks and scaffolds in place on the washer base, and paint the groove for the tracks black. Form and solder together the wire parts for the overhead sprayers. This assembly is attached by drilling $\frac{1}{8}$" deep holes where it meets the supports and base. Other pipes and valves to suit your particular layout can be added. For contrast I painted all the piping either gloss or flat black.

Finally, attach the track. You can do this several ways, depending on your own set-up. If you plan to add a new siding to accommodate the washer, simply run the track through the groove in the base and spike it down. Add enough gravel to the sides for adequate water drainage. If your track is already laid, and it is not convenient to take it up and slip the unit under it, cut the channel right off the base and put the washer on each side of the track in two sections.

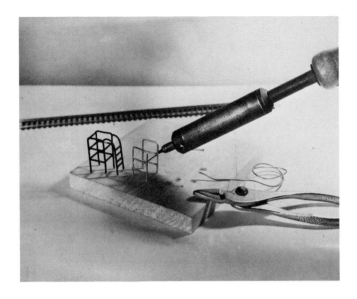

5 After you make the scaffold sides, stand them in holes in a piece of wood and solder cross pieces.

6 Add belt guards and motors to the ends of brush support arms; glue them well to insure strength.

7 Overhead water sprayers and nozzles are made from soft wire; fasten them in place with bent pins.

8 Make the scaffold floor from 1/16" balsa. Drill six holes in each walkway and insert the scaffolds.

9 Paint the washer light gray to simulate concrete and steel. The walks and scaffolds can be black.

10 The man on the scaffold with a window wiper is just the finishing touch for your model engine washer.

Bob Ferguson.

COALING STATION

BY ROBERT A. WHALEN

Drawings by Dick Wagner

YOU can build a model of the old New York Central coaling station at Harmon-on-Hudson, N. Y., for about $2. Harmon was the eastern terminal for steam locomotives of the NYC. The prototype coaling station is about 350 feet long, with 30 chutes on it. Here the Niagaras, some of the most highly advanced steam locomotives in American history, were refueled. Now this same chute is slowly deteriorating, for the diesel electrics that sounded the death knell for the mighty steam locomotives also doomed their servicing facilities as well. But if your model railroad still requires coaling stations, gather up the materials called for on page 47 and get to work. The step-by-step diagrams on the following pages explain the building procedures. In a few hours your engines can coal up at the newest facility on your pike.

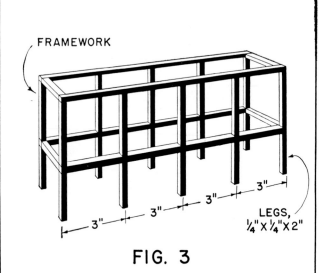

FRAMEWORK

3" 3" 3" 3"

LEGS,
¼"x¼"x2"

FIG. 3

CUT 10 PIECES OF ¼"x¼" BALSA STRIPPING, 2" LONG, FOR LEGS. CEMENT THE LEGS IN PLACE ON 3" CENTERS.

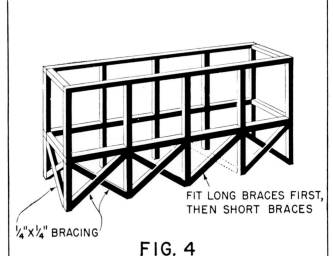

FIT LONG BRACES FIRST, THEN SHORT BRACES

¼"x¼" BRACING

FIG. 4

CUT DIAGONAL BRACES FROM ¼"x¼" BALSA STRIPPING. FIT AND CEMENT LONG BRACES FIRST, THEN SHORT BRACES. BRACING IS REQUIRED BETWEEN LEGS AT BOTH SIDES AND BOTH ENDS.

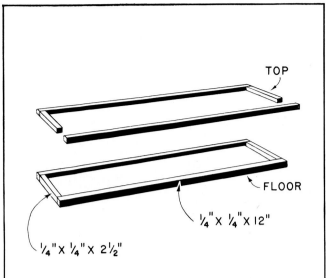

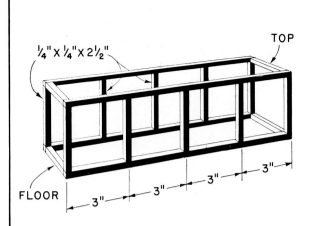

FIG. 1

CUT FOUR PIECES OF ¼" X ¼" BALSA STRIPPING, 12" LONG. CUT FOUR PIECES OF THE SAME MATERIAL, 2½" LONG. CEMENT TOGETHER AS SHOWN TO FORM TOP AND FLOOR OF BUILDING.

DIMENSIONS GIVEN ARE FOR HO SCALE. To build in O scale, multiply by 2 and subtract 10 per cent. For S scale, multiply by 1½ and subtract 10 per cent.

FIG. 2

CUT 10 PIECES OF ¼" X ¼" BALSA STRIPPING, 2½" LONG. CEMENT THESE 10 PIECES TO THE TOP AND FLOOR AS SHOWN TO FORM THE FRAMEWORK.

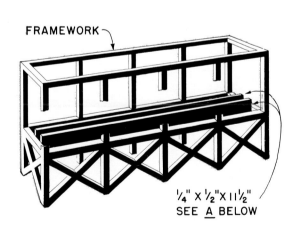

FIG. 5

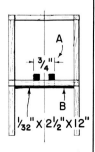

CUT TWO PIECES OF ¼" X ½" BALSA STRIPPING, 11½" LONG. CEMENT THEM IN PLACE AS SHOWN ABOVE AND AT <u>A</u>. NEXT, COVER BOTTOM OF FRAME WITH A PIECE OF ¹⁄₃₂" X 2½" X 12" BALSA SHEETING AS SHOWN AT <u>B</u>.

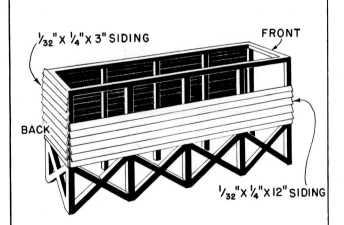

FIG. 6

CUT ¼" WIDE SIDING STRIPS FOR THE SIDES AND THE BACK WITH A STEEL RULER AND MODEL KNIFE FROM YOUR ¹⁄₃₂"X3"WIDE BALSA SHEETING. THE STRIPS ARE 12" LONG FOR THE SIDES AND 3"LONG FOR THE BACK. CEMENT BOTTOM STRIPS FIRST AND OVERLAP THE OTHER STRIPS UNTIL SIDES AND BACK ARE COVERED. LEAVE THE FRONT OPEN UNTIL LATER.

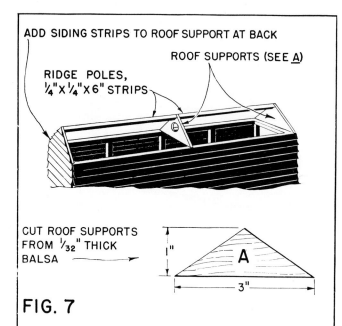

ADD SIDING STRIPS TO ROOF SUPPORT AT BACK

ROOF SUPPORTS (SEE <u>A</u>)

RIDGE POLES, ¼" x ¼" x 6" STRIPS

CUT ROOF SUPPORTS FROM ¹⁄₃₂" THICK BALSA

A

1"

3"

FIG. 7

CUT THREE ROOF SUPPORTS FROM ¹⁄₃₂" THICK BALSA SHEETING AS SHOWN AT A. CEMENT ONE AT THE FRONT, ONE AT THE CENTER AND ONE AT THE BACK. CUT TWO 6" RIDGE POLES FROM ¼" x ¼" STRIPPING. SAND THEM TO FIT BETWEEN THE ROOF SUPPORTS AND CEMENT IN PLACE. ADD SIDING STRIPS TO BACK AS INDICATED ABOVE. CUT HOLE IN CENTER SUPPORT FOR LAMP IF INTERIOR LIGHTING IS WANTED.

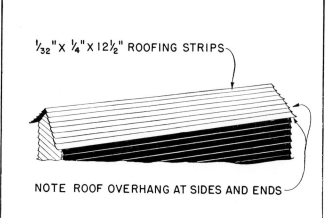

¹⁄₃₂" X ¼" X 12½" ROOFING STRIPS

NOTE ROOF OVERHANG AT SIDES AND ENDS

FIG. 8

CUT THE ROOFING FROM THE SAME SHEETING YOU USED FOR THE SIDING, MAKING THE ¼" STRIPS 12½" LONG TO ALLOW FOR OVERHANG AT BOTH ENDS. CEMENT FIRST STRIP SO IT OVERHANGS THE SIDE. CEMENT SUCCEEDING STRIPS IN PLACE, OVERLAPPING THEM IN THE SAME MANNER AS THE SIDING AND WORKING UPWARD TO THE RIDGE POLE. REPEAT ON OTHER SIDE.

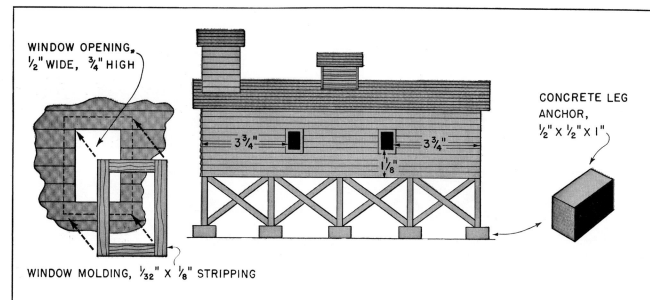

WINDOW OPENING, ½" WIDE, ¾" HIGH

3¾"

3¾"

⅛"

CONCRETE LEG ANCHOR, ½" X ½" X 1"

WINDOW MOLDING, ¹⁄₃₂" X ⅛" STRIPPING

FIG. 11

CUT TWO WINDOW OPENINGS IN EACH SIDE OF BUILDING AS INDICATED ABOVE. LOCATIONS OF WINDOWS ARE INDICATED ON THE PLAN; SIZE OF WINDOWS SHOWN ABOVE. CUT WINDOW MOLDING STRIPS ⅛" WIDE FROM ¹⁄₃₂" SHEETING AND CEMENT IN PLACE.

FIG. 12

YOU NEED 16 CONCRETE LEG ANCHORS. CUT THEM FROM ½" x ½" BALSA STRIPPING. CEMENT A LEG ANCHOR TO EACH LEG OF BUILDING. SET ASIDE THE OTHER SIX LEG ANCHORS FOR THE RAMP.

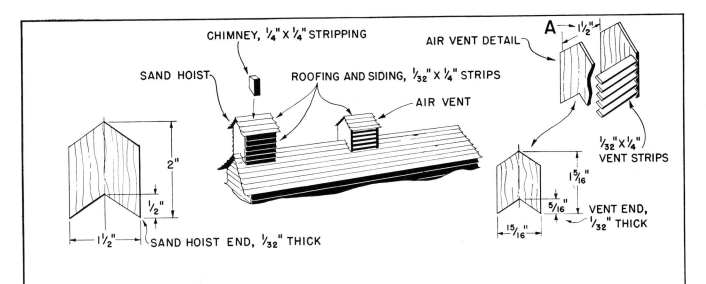

CHIMNEY, ¼" X ¼" STRIPPING

SAND HOIST

ROOFING AND SIDING, ⅟₃₂" X ¼" STRIPS

AIR VENT

AIR VENT DETAIL

A ←1½"→

⅟₃₂" X ¼"
VENT STRIPS

2"

½"

1½"

SAND HOIST END, ⅟₃₂" THICK

1⁵⁄₁₆"

⁵⁄₁₆"

VENT END,
⅟₃₂" THICK

15⁄₁₆"

FIG. 9

FIG. 10

NEXT COMES THE SAND HOIST. CUT TWO ENDS FROM ⅟₃₂" SHEETING AS SHOWN ABOVE. CEMENT THEM TO THE ROOF 1½" APART AS SHOWN AT A, FIG. 10. CUT SIDING AND ROOFING STRIPS FROM ⅟₃₂" SHEETING AND CEMENT THEM IN PLACE. BE SURE TO ALLOW FOR ROOF OVERHANG. CUT CHIMNEY FROM ¼" X ¼" STRIPPING AND CEMENT IN PLACE.

THE AIR VENT IS SIMILAR TO THE SAND HOIST AND IS CEMENTED IN PLACE AT THE EXACT CENTER OF THE ROOF. CUT TWO ENDS FROM ⅟₃₂" SHEETING. THE VENT SLATS OR STRIPS ARE CUT FROM ⅟₃₂" SHEETING. MOUNT VENT ENDS FIRST, 1½" APART (SEE A), THEN VENT STRIPS. LAST, APPLY ROOFING STRIPS; ALLOW FOR OVERHANG.

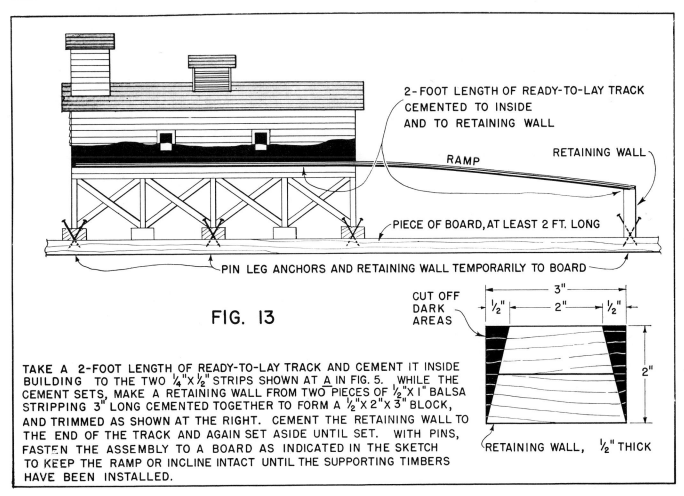

2-FOOT LENGTH OF READY-TO-LAY TRACK
CEMENTED TO INSIDE
AND TO RETAINING WALL

RAMP

RETAINING WALL

PIECE OF BOARD, AT LEAST 2 FT. LONG

PIN LEG ANCHORS AND RETAINING WALL TEMPORARILY TO BOARD

FIG. 13

CUT OFF
DARK
AREAS

3"

½" | 2" | ½"

2"

RETAINING WALL, ½" THICK

TAKE A 2-FOOT LENGTH OF READY-TO-LAY TRACK AND CEMENT IT INSIDE BUILDING TO THE TWO ¼" X ½" STRIPS SHOWN AT A IN FIG. 5. WHILE THE CEMENT SETS, MAKE A RETAINING WALL FROM TWO PIECES OF ½" X 1" BALSA STRIPPING 3" LONG CEMENTED TOGETHER TO FORM A ½" X 2" X 3" BLOCK, AND TRIMMED AS SHOWN AT THE RIGHT. CEMENT THE RETAINING WALL TO THE END OF THE TRACK AND AGAIN SET ASIDE UNTIL SET. WITH PINS, FASTEN THE ASSEMBLY TO A BOARD AS INDICATED IN THE SKETCH TO KEEP THE RAMP OR INCLINE INTACT UNTIL THE SUPPORTING TIMBERS HAVE BEEN INSTALLED.

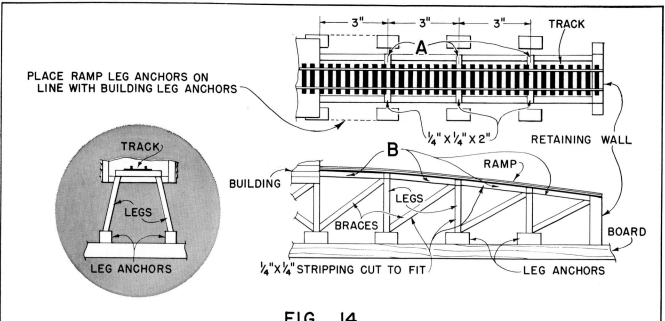

PLACE RAMP LEG ANCHORS ON LINE WITH BUILDING LEG ANCHORS

TRACK — 3" — 3" — 3" — TRACK

A

¼" X ¼" X 2"   RETAINING WALL

TRACK

LEGS

LEG ANCHORS

BUILDING — B — RAMP

LEGS

BRACES

BOARD

¼" X ¼" STRIPPING CUT TO FIT   LEG ANCHORS

FIG. 14

ALL THE SUPPORTING TIMBERS OF THE RAMP ARE CUT FROM ¼" X ¼" STRIPPING. FIRST, CUT THREE 2-INCH PIECES AND CEMENT THEM IN PLACE TO THE TIES OF THE RAMP TRACK AS SHOWN AT A. NOTE THAT THESE STRIPS ARE ON 3-INCH CENTERS. PIN THE LEG ANCHORS TEMPORARILY TO THE BOARD ON LINE WITH BUILDING LEG ANCHORS AND ON THE SAME 3-INCH CENTERS AS THE STRIPS AT A. NEXT, CUT THREE PAIRS OF LEGS TO FIT BETWEEN THE STRIPS AT A AND THE LEG ANCHORS AND CEMENT THEM IN PLACE. CUT STRIPS SHOWN AT B AND DIAGONAL BRACES AND CEMENT THEM IN PLACE. WHEN THE CEMENT HAS SET, REMOVE THE PINS FROM THE LEG ANCHORS AND THE RAMP WILL HOLD ITS SHAPE.

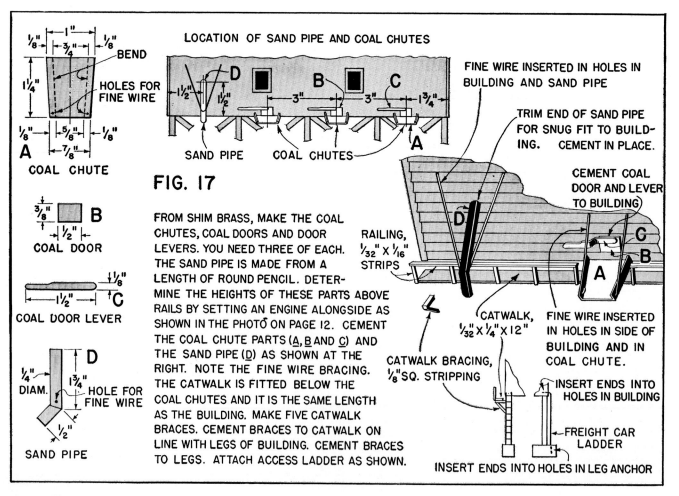

LOCATION OF SAND PIPE AND COAL CHUTES

⅛" — 1" — ⅛"
— ¾" —
BEND
1¼"
HOLES FOR FINE WIRE
⅛" — ⅝" — ⅛"
— ⅞" —
A
COAL CHUTE

1½" — 1½" — 3" — 3" — 1¾"
D   B   C
SAND PIPE   COAL CHUTES   A

FINE WIRE INSERTED IN HOLES IN BUILDING AND SAND PIPE

TRIM END OF SAND PIPE FOR SNUG FIT TO BUILD-ING. CEMENT IN PLACE.

CEMENT COAL DOOR AND LEVER TO BUILDING)

FIG. 17

⅜" — ½" — B
COAL DOOR

⅛"
1½" — C
COAL DOOR LEVER

D
¼" DIAM.
1¾"
HOLE FOR FINE WIRE
½"
SAND PIPE

FROM SHIM BRASS, MAKE THE COAL CHUTES, COAL DOORS AND DOOR LEVERS. YOU NEED THREE OF EACH. THE SAND PIPE IS MADE FROM A LENGTH OF ROUND PENCIL. DETER-MINE THE HEIGHTS OF THESE PARTS ABOVE RAILS BY SETTING AN ENGINE ALONGSIDE AS SHOWN IN THE PHOTO ON PAGE 12. CEMENT THE COAL CHUTE PARTS (A, B AND C) AND THE SAND PIPE (D) AS SHOWN AT THE RIGHT. NOTE THE FINE WIRE BRACING. THE CATWALK IS FITTED BELOW THE COAL CHUTES AND IT IS THE SAME LENGTH AS THE BUILDING. MAKE FIVE CATWALK BRACES. CEMENT BRACES TO CATWALK ON LINE WITH LEGS OF BUILDING. CEMENT BRACES TO LEGS. ATTACH ACCESS LADDER AS SHOWN.

RAILING, 1/32" X 1/16" STRIPS

D

CATWALK, 1/32" X ¼" X 12"

CATWALK BRACING, ⅛" SQ. STRIPPING

C
B
A

FINE WIRE INSERTED IN HOLES IN SIDE OF BUILDING AND IN COAL CHUTE.

INSERT ENDS INTO HOLES IN BUILDING

FREIGHT CAR LADDER

INSERT ENDS INTO HOLES IN LEG ANCHOR

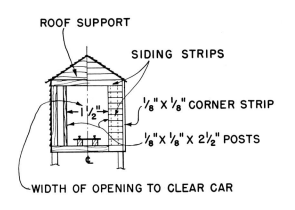

ROOF SUPPORT

SIDING STRIPS

1/8" X 1/8" CORNER STRIP

1/8" X 1/8" X 2 1/2" POSTS

WIDTH OF OPENING TO CLEAR CAR

FIG. 15

LET'S FINISH THE FRONT OF THE BUILDING. CUT TWO 1/8" X 1/8" POSTS 2 1/2" LONG AND CEMENT THEM IN PLACE AS SHOWN ABOVE. CUT SIDING STRIPS FROM 1/32" BALSA SHEETING THE SAME AS FOR THE BACK. SEE FIG. 6. CUT 3/4" LENGTH STRIPS TO FIT EITHER SIDE OF THE OPENING. CEMENT THEM IN PLACE, STARTING AT THE BOTTOM AND WORKING UPWARD. CUT STRIPS OVER OPENING TO FIT SLOPING ROOF AND CEMENT IN PLACE. FINISH CORNERS OF CHUTE WITH 1/8" X 1/8" STRIPS.

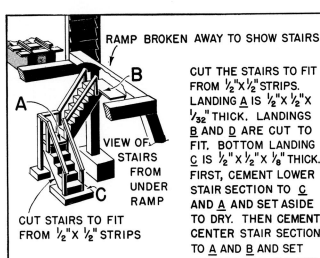

RAMP BROKEN AWAY TO SHOW STAIRS

B

A

VIEW OF STAIRS FROM UNDER RAMP

C

CUT STAIRS TO FIT FROM 1/2" X 1/2" STRIPS

FIG. 16

CUT THE STAIRS TO FIT FROM 1/2" X 1/2" STRIPS. LANDING A IS 1/2" X 1/2" X 1/32" THICK. LANDINGS B AND D ARE CUT TO FIT. BOTTOM LANDING C IS 1/2" X 1/2" X 1/8" THICK. FIRST, CEMENT LOWER STAIR SECTION TO C AND A AND SET ASIDE TO DRY. THEN CEMENT CENTER STAIR SECTION TO A AND B AND SET ASIDE TO DRY. CUT RAILING STRIPS FROM 1/32" SHEETING, 1/16" WIDE. TRIM TO FIT AND CEMENT IN PLACE. CEMENT STAIRS IN PLACE AS SHOWN. FINISH THE STAIRS AS SHOWN AT THE LEFT. CEMENT RAILING IN PLACE AT SIDE AND ALONG RAMP.

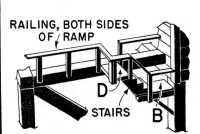

RAILING, BOTH SIDES OF RAMP

D

STAIRS

B

VIEW OF STAIRS FROM SIDE OF RAMP

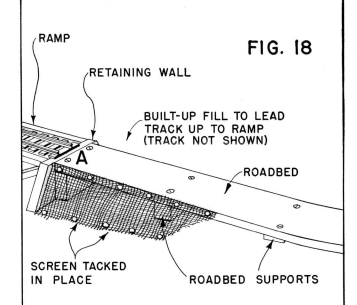

RAMP

FIG. 18

RETAINING WALL

BUILT-UP FILL TO LEAD TRACK UP TO RAMP (TRACK NOT SHOWN)

A

ROADBED

SCREEN TACKED IN PLACE

ROADBED SUPPORTS

TO FINISH OUR COALING STATION, WE MUST EXTEND OUR TRACK FROM THE END OF THE RAMP TO THE GROUND LEVEL. ONE WAY TO DO THIS IS SHOWN ABOVE. INSTALL ROADBED AND TRACK, THE SAME KINDS AS ON THE REST OF YOUR PIKE. IF YOU USE THE TYPE OF ROADBED WITH TIES, MAKE SURE THE TIES ARE EVEN WITH THOSE ON THE RAMP AT A. TACK SCREENING IN PLACE, ADD PLASTER "EARTH" AND PAINT WHEN SET. PAINT THE COALING STATION BLACK. LEG ANCHORS AND RETAINING WALL ARE GRAY.

BILL OF MATERIALS
(HO gauge)

Balsa sheeting:

9 feet, 1/32" x 3".

Balsa stripping:

2 feet, 1/8" x 1/8";

25 feet, 1/4" x 1/4";

6 feet, 1/2" x 1/2";

6", 1/2" x 1", or equivalent.

Grain o' wheat bulb.

Flexible rail: 3 feet.

Glossy black paint: 1 bottle.

Glue: 2 tubes.

Ladder stripping: 1 foot, ready-made.

Shim brass: 6", .005" sheet.

Fine wire: 2 feet.

Round pencil: 3", 1/4" diameter.

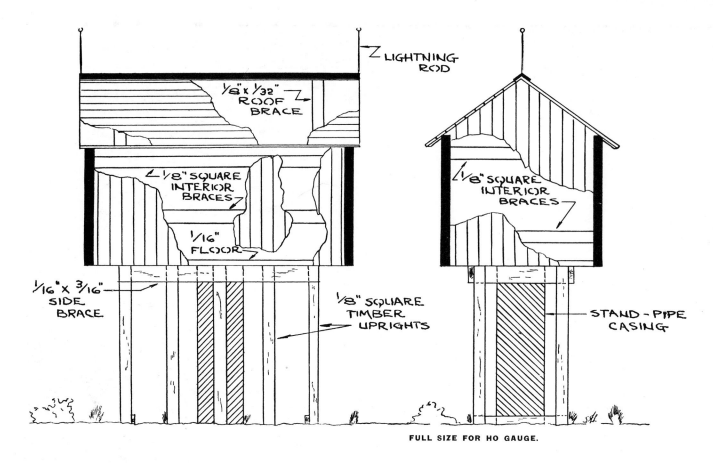

FULL SIZE FOR HO GAUGE.

ATMOSPHERE FROM THE NINETIES

A rectangular water tank

BY J. A. LUKAS

HERE is a little structure that will take you back to the Gay Nineties. It can be built in a comparatively short time and will give atmosphere to the branch line that goes off into the hills or add a bit of extra charm to your main line. A similar prototype of this model may be found at the Virginia & Truckee Carson City yard, if it hasn't been torn down by now.

I altered my model slightly by eliminating the spouts. These would normally be on each end, but since I located my model on a slight rise of ground a short distance from a yard, the spouts would have been useless. In their place I substituted a water column at trackside.

Now for the actual construction. The HO model is fabricated for the most part of ⅛" x 1/32" basswood strips and ⅛"-square pine stringers. Cut 44 basswood strips 1⅜" x ⅛" x 1/32"; these

will be used to form the sides of the tank. Next cut the end strips, 26 in all, but be sure to allow for additional length because of the slope of the roof on either side. For actual dimensions, consult the full-size end elevation.

You will need ten 3" x ⅛" x 1/32" basswood strips to construct the roof. Consult the bracing detail diagram to see the method by which sides, ends and roof are brought to completion. Use the ⅛"-square pine stringers to brace the different assemblies. Pin down the ⅛" stringers in pairs, being careful to adhere to the spacing dimensions shown in the diagram. Now cement the 1⅜" x ⅛" x 1/32" planking to the braces at perfect right angles, 22 planks per side. Follow the same method for the ends: 13 planks per end and 5 planks for each roof half. After these assemblies have thoroughly dried, cut the excess stringer flush to the last plank in all cases.

Now that you have completed the

side, end and roof assemblies, proceed to lay out the floor. Cut it from one piece of a 1/16"-thick section of sheet pine. It will measure 2¾" in length and 1 9/16" in width.

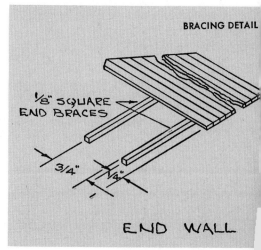

BRACING DETAIL

⅛" SQUARE END BRACES

3/4"

¼"

END WALL

At this point assemble the tank itself. This is done by first setting the 1/16" x 2¾" x 1⁹/₁₆" pine floor on a small piece of wax paper. This prevents the structure from sticking when it is cemented. Now cement the two sides and ends around the floor. Also, apply cement to the four corners. Keep an eye on this to make sure the structure sets right; both sides and ends must be at 90° angles to the base and properly aligned.

Notch the side walls in two places at the top of the walls. These notches will be ⅛" in width and ¹/₃₂" thick, and ⁵/₁₆" in from both ends on each side. This is done to receive the two braces that support the roof planks. There will be a 1/16" overhang of the roof at each end after these assemblies are set into the proper position.

The major portion of the tank is finished. Now add the trim on the corners. This is shown in black on the side-and-end elevation diagram. There will be two to a corner; cut them from the same ⅛" x ¹/₃₂" basswood strips you used for the side planks. Fasten these to the four corners and an additional pair to the roof. After they have been added, the superstructure is complete except for the final sanding.

The standpipe casing is also constructed of 1/16" sheet pine. Cut four 1⅝" x ½" x 1/16" sides and cement these to form the assembly. Now thoroughly sand the tank structure and standpipe casing, using 00 paper. Brush several coats of wood sealer over the water tank between sandings to get a smooth surface for painting.

Next you need 10 timber uprights for the water tank supporting structure; these should be ⅛" x ⅛" x 1⅝". First cut the two upright top supports to size: 2⅛" x ³/₁₆" x 1/16". Gather five of the timber uprights and cement them to the top support, being careful to keep them at right angles to the support. Also, be sure to space the

Nezih Manyas.

This is the author's model of the rather unusual rectangular water tank he once saw in the Carson City yard of the Virginia & Truckee. He eliminated spouts on each end of the tank and substituted a water column at trackside.

uprights at the proper distance from each other. Take these dimensions directly from the elevations.

Now cement the uprights on the other side to the top support in the same way. By looking at the elevations again you will observe four additional braces on the tank supporting structure. There are two braces at the top and two at the bottom on each end of this structure. These are 1" x ³/₁₆" x 1/16" and are cemented into position. This is accomplished by standing both rows of uprights up and cementing the braces in their desired positions simultaneously. Sand this structure several

times and use wood sealer as you did before.

Now position the water tank superstructure squarely over the supporting uprights and cement these two assemblies together. Cement the standpipe casing in position squarely in the center of the tank as shown by the photo and diagram.

Now your model is ready for the painters. I'd suggest painting the corner and roof trim a light color and the remainder of the model a contrasting shade, or the reverse of this. However, the final decision for that matter is always up to the builder.

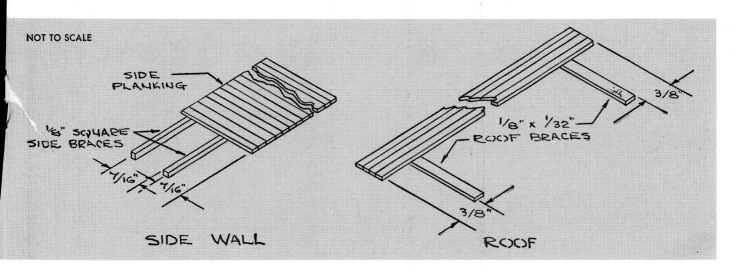

NOT TO SCALE

SIDE PLANKING

⅛" SQUARE SIDE BRACES

7/16"   7/16"

SIDE WALL

⅛" x ¹/₃₂"
ROOF BRACES

3/8"

3/8"

ROOF

Superdetail a kit-built water tank

BY BILL McCLANAHAN

Photos by Clint Grant

NO DOUBT if you've been in the model railroad business long enough to get your feet really wet, you have some old kit-built structures which you assembled in your apprentice days that no longer seem to fit into the scheme of things. Yet, possibly for sentiment's sake, you're a little hesitant about throwing away an old model. You salve your conscience by relegating it to the background or some other inconspicuous spot where it will cover up bare space, yet won't be too noticeable.

Such was the case on my Texas & Rio Grande Western. I had an old Skyline water tank which I bought immediately after the end of World War II, when I started model railroading. The vertical scribing representing the wooden tank sides and the tank hoops were both printed on a paper wrapper which was pasted around the cardboard tube which served as the tank. Naturally they lacked a three-dimensional quality. Yet the base of the tank seemed attractive enough. The model as a whole, however, stood out in poor taste among the rest of my structures, which are mostly scratch-built. It seemed to lack realism.

I got to thinking one day: would it be possible to improve a model structure without the tedious task of completely tearing it apart and starting from the beginning? The answer is clearly shown in the accompanying photographs.

The tank as assembled originally from kit instructions appears toylike. See photo below, left. Compare it with the revised version on the next page. In rebuilding it my aim was to make an old weather-beaten tank that had become smoked and weather-stained after years of giving long drinks of water to passing locomotives. Actually the transition was not a rebuilding job. Rather, I took up the construction where I left off years ago and added detail.

From the original structure I removed only three things, as shown in the photo below, right: the spout and its unrealistic hanger rope, the ladder and the water-level indicator. That photo also shows the first step in adding detail. Nothing looks more like real wood sides than real wood, so I cut a new tank wrapper from 1/32"-thick Northeastern scale scribed siding. The scribing should be vertical.

Since this scribed siding was not available in a width that enabled me to cut a wrapper all in one piece, it was necessary to cut about three sections and fit them in place around the tank. I coated these sections liberally with cement and held them in place with several rubber bands. While the cement was drying (I usually let such a job set overnight), I went on to the next step. The kit roof was slick and unrealistic, and after the new siding was in place, the eaves didn't extend far enough over the tank sides.

I built the new roof directly on top of the old. You can cut it from three-ply Strathmore illustration board, but comparable stock will work fine. The simplest way to do this is to determine the radius of the old tank roof and draw a circle on the Strathmore board to that radius. Then measure the front edge, Z, of one of the pie-shaped roof sections as shown in Fig. 1. Extend this radius anywhere from 3/16" to 1/4", depending upon how much more overhang is desired, and draw a concentric circle around your original roof circle. Extend radius lines X and Y to touch the circumference of the new circle and then join these points. Now you have the pattern ready

The author's original kit-built tank.

First step: use scribed siding to make a new and realistic tank wrapper.

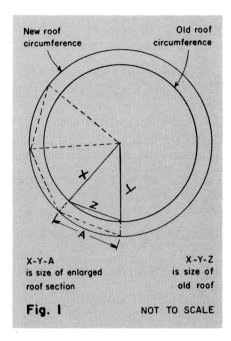

New roof circumference   Old roof circumference

X-Y-A
is size of enlarged
roof section

X-Y-Z
is size of
old roof

Fig. 1   NOT TO SCALE

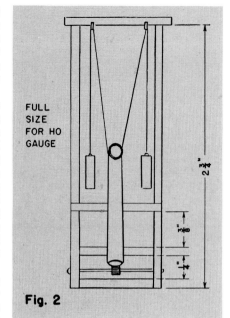

FULL
SIZE
FOR HO
GAUGE

Fig. 2

for the new and larger roof sections.

Cut the new roof all in one piece, scribing and bending at the proper radius lines, or cut it in separate pie-shaped pieces. In any event, be sure to cement the new roof directly to the old roof.

If you are in a hurry and don't care for the tedious job of laying a shingled roof, your new roof covering may be sandpaper to represent a gravel-on-tar roof. Or you may lay strips of crinkled masking tape and paint it black to represent a tarpaper roof.

I wanted an old weather-beaten shingled roof. Shingles can be cut from card stock and notched and laid in strips. I used actual cedar shingles cut from some of that thin sheet cedar that comes wrapped around certain makes of cigars. Remove the cedar wrapper from the cigar, iron it flat with a warm iron and cut the strips across the grain after notching.

If you choose a shingle roof, it will be necessary to put ridge planks along the edge of each section. I made mine of 3/16" wide Strathmore strips, scored and bent to lap over the ridge of each section.

The hatch on the roof is a piece of 1/2"-square scribed siding. In place of a pointed finial in the center of the roof, I placed one of those shirt pins with a round ball on the end.

When the roof is completed, it's time to attach the tank hoops. I made mine of soft iron wire. The hoops are spaced closer together at the bottom of the tank and grow farther apart as they near the top. Since this is supposed to be an old weather-beaten tank that has been in use a long time, it isn't too important that the hoops be absolutely straight and true to a 90-degree angle to the siding scribing.

In most old tanks, some of the hoops have loosened and slipped, so if your hoops are a bit askew, that lends to the over-all effect of aging and decay you want in the tank. Twist the hoops as tightly as possible about the tank and solder the twisted ends.

In this detailing project the spout hanger is an important addition. It is constructed of Ayres 8" x 8" scale stripwood as shown in Fig. 2. I used the kit spout and hinged it on a long dressmaker's pin (a strip of wire works fine) which I drove through the bottom of the hanger. Then I looped heavy thread (a light bit of fishing line will do) around the end of the spout, cemented it in place, and threaded the two ends through eye bolts at the top of the hanger.

Actually, on the prototype these lines or cables work through a pulley at the top of the hanger, but I have yet to see a scale working pulley in HO, so I substituted the eye bolts made from a common pin and driven into the hanger. It's best to fasten the hanger to the tank side before attempting this operation. The sharp ends of the eye bolts are driven through the hanger into the side of the tank, adding to the strength of the construction.

I made the counterweights at the ends of the spout lines from strips of 1/4" solid spool solder. I didn't attach the ladder and water-level indicator until after the tank had been weathered and stained.

I painted my tank with a water-thin stain of oil paints, using Van Dyke brown, raw umber and burnt umber, with just a spot of green flowed in to represent mold or mildew. About the same effect can be achieved using model railroad lacquer, in box car red, brown, black and yellow, thinned down with lacquer thinner. After the staining is dry, the finishing touch is to add alkaline white stains by dry-brushing streaks of white vertically on the tank sides.

Place lichen and other small bits of model railroad shrubbery around the base to complete the model.

Basically it's the same water tank, but superdetailing makes the difference.

Balsa or scale siding can be used to build this superintendent's office. It's a good structure for a small road.

SMALL STRUCTURE FOR A SMALL SPACE

Division superintendent's office and storeroom

BY JOE WILHELM

Photos by the author

This cistern is placed alongside the building to catch and store rain water.

WHEN I pick a structure for my pike, I try to keep in mind that compared to prototype railroads, I'm badly pressed for space. Even the largest model railroads are no more than pinhead size when we compare the miles of prototype right of way with the inches we have. Suppose your layout is four feet wide—in HO gauge, that means 348 scale feet wide. That's about the size of one city block. If you have a layout 32 actual feet long, that's about eight blocks long in HO scale. You can walk that in a few minutes, but in a layout it has to represent entire countrysides. You also know 32 feet of layout is quite exceptional.

Here is a very small structure designed to fit between tracks. It serves as both a storeroom and as an office for the division superintendent and his staff. It will not be out of place on the smallest layout. Also, it is easy to build; any newcomer to the hobby should be able to complete it in two or three evenings of work.

Construction

I used my own method of construction on this building, a method I don't recall ever seeing described. If you do not wish to follow my ideas, then build it with Northeastern siding and scale lumber, which is easy to handle and truly beautiful material. Whichever method you choose, you will find this a good project and one that will give you many interesting construction hours.

Take your time on this building, and do your best. If you are a new model builder, follow the directions closely; if an old-timer, then just use the drawings. Here goes!

Use the templates, which you will find on the next page, to cut out the sides, roof pieces, track end and the front from 1/32" sheet balsa. Cut window and door openings. Now, with 1/8" balsa, make a floor piece which will fit inside the bottom edge of the four upright pieces when they are together. I have shown no template for this; it will vary according to differences in your accuracy of cutting, so it is much easier to fit by trial and error.

Now, while the sides are still able to be laid flat on the workbench, press in the weatherboarding. Notice in the drawing on the next page how the X-acto knife is held at an angle to do the job. Do not cut; just pressure will flatten the wood quite well. Refer to the drawings at the right to see how high the weatherboarding goes. The track end is completely weatherboarded. The upper parts are finished by gluing slivers of balsa, cut with a razor blade and steel rule,

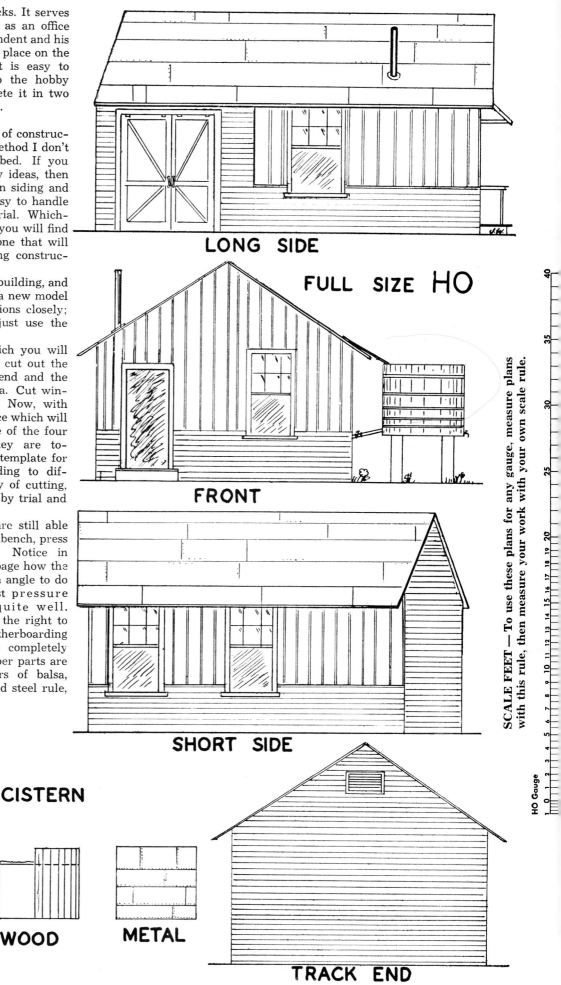

LONG SIDE

FULL SIZE HO

FRONT

SHORT SIDE

CISTERN

WOOD

METAL

TRACK END

SCALE FEET — To use these plans for any gauge, measure plans with this rule, then measure your work with your own scale rule.

HO Gauge

Terminal and Yard Facilities   53

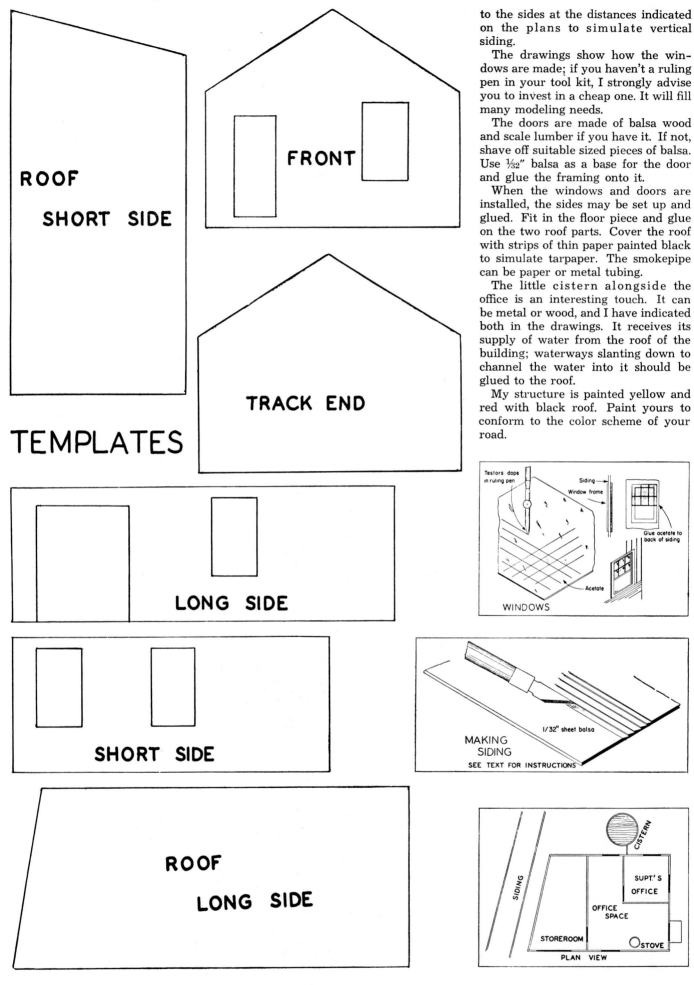

ROOF
SHORT SIDE

FRONT

TRACK END

TEMPLATES

LONG SIDE

SHORT SIDE

ROOF
LONG SIDE

to the sides at the distances indicated on the plans to simulate vertical siding.

The drawings show how the windows are made; if you haven't a ruling pen in your tool kit, I strongly advise you to invest in a cheap one. It will fill many modeling needs.

The doors are made of balsa wood and scale lumber if you have it. If not, shave off suitable sized pieces of balsa. Use 1/32" balsa as a base for the door and glue the framing onto it.

When the windows and doors are installed, the sides may be set up and glued. Fit in the floor piece and glue on the two roof parts. Cover the roof with strips of thin paper painted black to simulate tarpaper. The smokepipe can be paper or metal tubing.

The little cistern alongside the office is an interesting touch. It can be metal or wood, and I have indicated both in the drawings. It receives its supply of water from the roof of the building; waterways slanting down to channel the water into it should be glued to the roof.

My structure is painted yellow and red with black roof. Paint yours to conform to the color scheme of your road.

Testors dope in ruling pen

Siding
Window frame
Glue acetate to back of siding
Acetate
WINDOWS

1/32" sheet balsa
MAKING SIDING
SEE TEXT FOR INSTRUCTIONS

CISTERN
SIDING
SUPT'S OFFICE
OFFICE SPACE
STOREROOM
STOVE
PLAN VIEW

A scale scale house

BY DONALD SIMS

Photos by the author

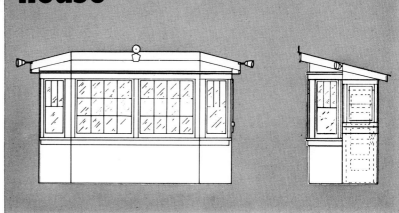

To use these plans for other gauges, measure the plans with an HO scale rule and measure your work with the proper rule for your own gauge.

IF bulk commodities are a part of your railroad's freight tonnage, then you're in the market for a scale house. Just about every road can use one. The model shown belongs to the Trona Railway, a 30-mile California short line that mainly handles bulk chemicals. Of course, a scale house can also weigh box cars or whatever type of freight equipment that's built. Any time a railroad has to weigh a car, it goes to the nearest scale house.

Trona Railway's scale house is easily duplicated as a model. Functionally it is a protective shed built around a large weighing machine. The main construction material is corrugated sheet metal. Sides, ends and the roof can be cut from any stock which duplicates its appearance. Balsawood can be used to simulate beams which support the roof and the outside trimming just underneath. Window frames and sashes are similarly made.

Both ends of the shed are equipped with large floodlights for night operation. The person weighing cars must be able to see numbers and other data on car sides, hence the lighting. For an added note of realism you might try a couple of small bulbs on the model. There's plenty of room inside the building to hide the wiring.

You'll need two dummy switch stands, plus some odds and ends of rail, to fix up a separate track for the scale house. The object is to get cars on the weighing machine, which has a track of its own. The twin ribbons are laid down alongside the lead track, with only a short space intervening between each rail. They almost give the appearance of guard rails. The switches can be of a workable variety.

Balsawood comes in for more usage on the long platform that fronts Trona's scale house. Those 1/16"-square stringers that can be picked up in a hobby shop will make realistic-looking boards. Sixty scale feet of platform is built up from the stringers. In width, there should be enough to cover all space between rails plus an 18" overhang on each side. A smaller platform at the shed's base calls for wider boards, as on the prototype.

A yard location would be the most logical place to install your completed scale house. Scales are usually found at one end of a yard where a lead track is nearby. Or if your pike has an industry that originates a steady stream of car loadings, such as coal or cement, that would make an excellent choice too. As far as Trona Railway's prototype goes, it's a little of both. The scale house is in a yard, but it's also close to a chemical plant that uses covered hoppers for bulk loading.

As a final tip, try scattering some coal or cement (or whatever commodity is going to be weighed) on the tracks around the scale house. Bulk-loaded cars have a habit of spilling some of their contents along the roadbed. Some spilled material lying around will dispel the antiseptic look that characterizes too many models. After all, you have a working model, not a piece of equipment all dolled up to pass the board of directors.

Corrugated sides and large windows on the prototype can be duplicated with ease on a model. Floodlights are a must on a scale house, which often works 'round the clock.

Place the scale house in a setting like that on the Trona Railway. The weighing machine has its own track; you can lay odd pieces in position alongside the lead track.

Terminal and Yard Facilities 55

Here's how the section tool house looks when it is set down in the scenic surroundings of a railroad. The base fits snugly against the roadbed and the track.

ROOM FOR TWO SCOOTERS

A section tool house

BY ROBERT E. GILBERT

Photo and drawings by the author

FIND a spot on your railroad for a section tool house. You see many of these structures on prototype railroads; they usually abut on the main line and are often found in rural districts. The HO model I built for the Razorback-East Grimalkin follows a Clinchfield prototype in the yards at Erwin, Tenn. The design is distinctive. There are three double doors; tracks run into the two outside partitions that house the section cars and the center door leads to a room that holds tools and supplies. You can arrange an interesting scene around this building with barrels, boxes and old ties scattered about, handcars or motorized section cars in the doorways, and section hands at work.

Begin construction with the base and floor, which is a single unit made to imitate the prototype. As you can see in the side-view drawing, the model is designed to fit against a main line consisting of Atlas curvable track laid on Tru-Scale plain roadbed. If you are building in S or O scale, or if you have another type of HO track, make any necessary adjustments to keep the mainline rails and the section car rails level. The easiest way to do this is to change the thickness of the bottom section of the base. The complete base is 5/16" thick. Measure the

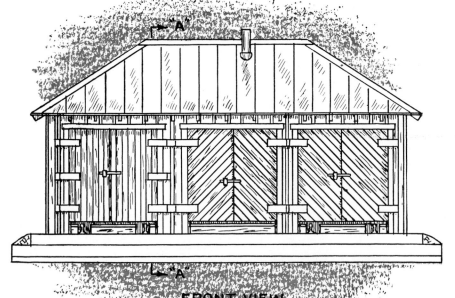

FRONT VIEW

HO Gauge

SCALE FEET — To use these plans for any gauge, measure plans with this rule, then measure your work with your own scale rule.

thickness of your roadbed and add the thickness of the ties to see if this figure is correct in your case.

Cut out the top, center and bottom base sections as shown on page 61. Use ⅛" plywood for the top and center sections, and ¹⁄₁₆" wood for the bottom. Cement eight piles, about 12" in diameter, to the bottom section as shown in the drawing. These piles should be ⅛" thick, so cement cubes of ⅛" wood in place and then cut the cubes to a round shape.

Cement the center section to the bottom with the front edges in line. Strengthen the joint by driving in spikes or tiny nails with the heads flush. Space the top section 18" from each side of the center section and let it overhang 15" in front.

On the top section, draw the two center lines for the section car tracks. You need four rails, each 25 feet long; scraps of rail will do fine for these tracks. Secure them, in gauge, on each side of the center lines so that they extend 2'-6" beyond the front of the base. I used Pliobond cement to hold them down.

Next, fabricate the five floor parts detailed on the plan. Scribe ³⁄₃₂" spaces on ¹⁄₃₂"-thick balsa. Cement these parts to ¹⁄₁₆" balsa of the same dimensions. Fasten the floor pieces to the base, aligning them with the back edge of the top section.

To complete the base and floor, round out the steplike contours of the base with scraps of balsa as shown in the drawing and in the front and side views. Stain the floor with a thin gray wash and paint the piles a brown creosote color.

Walls

Cut the walls (see pages 60 and 61) from ¹⁄₁₆" Northeastern capped siding with ⅛" spacing. In S or O scale, you may use the capped siding with ³⁄₁₆" spacing. You can also make your own capped siding by cementing strips of cardboard to wood.

All four walls may be constructed at once, but I'll describe the front wall first. The interior and exterior views are given in the plans. Since the siding material is 3½" wide, it is necessary to butt two pieces together to obtain the correct width.

All walls except the front one are 10'-6" high. The front wall is 9'-7" to allow for the thickness of the center base section. To get the required height, measure 10'-6" with a scale rule, then deduct a real ⅛".

I do not know why the prototype has three kinds of doors unevenly spaced, but it makes things interesting. The dimensions for the door openings are on the inside view. Work carefully while cutting these; if anything splits, use cement.

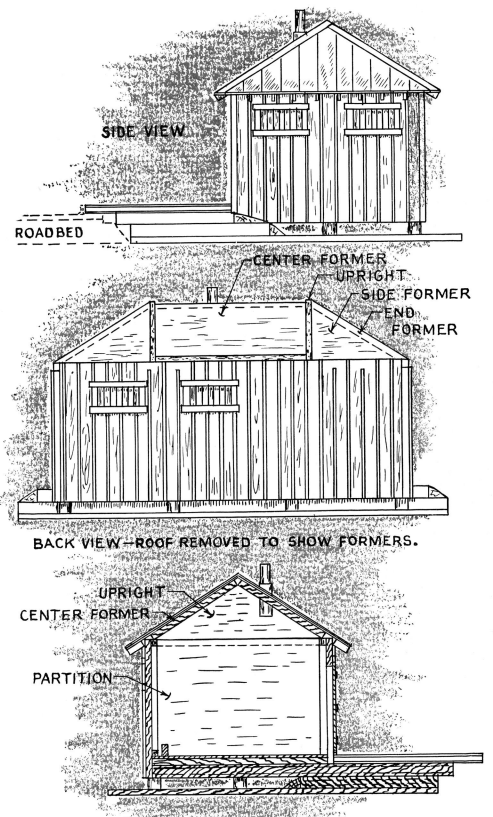

SIDE VIEW

ROADBED

CENTER FORMER
UPRIGHT
SIDE FORMER
END FORMER

BACK VIEW—ROOF REMOVED TO SHOW FORMERS.

UPRIGHT
CENTER FORMER
PARTITION

Turn this wall over and cut away any caps that will interfere with adding the ¹⁄₃₂" x ¹⁄₁₆" trim strips around the doorways. If you want contrasting trim, paint walls and strips before cementing them together. The prototype has gray walls and brown trim. Space the strips 1½" from the sides of the openings and 3" from the top. Notice that the trim above the openings extends 1½" beyond the side strips. There are also short ¹⁄₃₂" x ¹⁄₁₆" pieces beside the openings. Attach the hinges to these. Locate them by measuring down from the top trim strip. Turn the wall over and cement

¹⁄₁₆"-square bracing to the back of it.

The doors on the tool house (see page 61) are 3'-6" x 7'-0" and represent sheathing doors constructed by nailing two layers of planks together at right angles. For my HO model, I used ¹⁄₃₂"-thick Northeastern scribed sheathing with ¹⁄₁₆" spacing. Scribe the planks on the back, but take care in doing this since you will be working across the grain. For S or O scale, use Northeastern sheathing with ⅛" spacing. You can probably cement two layers together instead of scribing the back.

Two of the doors have the planks angled at 45 degrees. Use a triangle or a protractor to mark these on the wood. After the doors are cut, attach a ¹⁄₃₂" x ¹⁄₁₆" strip to one section of the left-hand door. Make 14 cloth hinges, 6" x 18". These are rather large, but they are durable. You may want to make them smaller in a larger scale. I cut mine from a form of picture hanger. The linen used for model airplane elevator hinges would also be good. Cement the hinges to the doors.

Bore holes for the latches in each door section. The working latches resemble those on the prototype and are sketched in the latch detail drawing, page 60. Each requires a model railroad spike and a pin. Cut off the spike about ¹⁄₁₆" below the head and cement it in the left-hand door section. Bend the pin as close to ¹⁄₃₂" below the head as you can. Cut off the point about 18 scale inches below the head. Push it through the door from inside and let it swing freely.

Paint the doors and then fasten them in place by cementing the hinges to the front wall. I made the hinges on my model stronger by coating them on the outside with Pliobond cement, which hardens into something like rubber.

For the back wall, cut out the window openings and trim them with strips cemented even with the edges; add ¹⁄₁₆" square bracing on the inside.

The two side walls are similar, except for the two trim strips at each edge. Cement one strip flush against the edge, and then let the other overlap it to form an angle around the corner. The strips should begin 7½" below the top of the wall to leave space for the false rafters on the roof. At the front corners of the building, stop the trim 12" above the bottom of the wall to prevent interference with the base. Make one side wall as shown on the plan, with the short strips at the left. Make the other wall with the strips at the right. See page 61.

Cut six shutters from Northeastern scribed sheathing. You may want to cement some of these in an open position, as if hinged at the top. Place the others in the openings even with the inside of the walls.

Roof

The hip roof has several parts. First there is the subroof of ¹⁄₁₆"-thick balsa formers. Cut the formers to the measurements given and bevel the edges where required to assure a smooth fit. While you are working with ¹⁄₁₆" balsa, make two supply-room partitions, 8'-9" x 13'-0", to go inside the main walls of the section tool house. Roof parts are on these pages.

The visible roof consists of four parts composed of a layer of shim aluminum and a layer of card stock about one scale inch thick. If no aluminum is handy, try empty toothpaste or shaving cream tubes as a substitute. Cut the tubes open, wash them and flatten then by rubbing

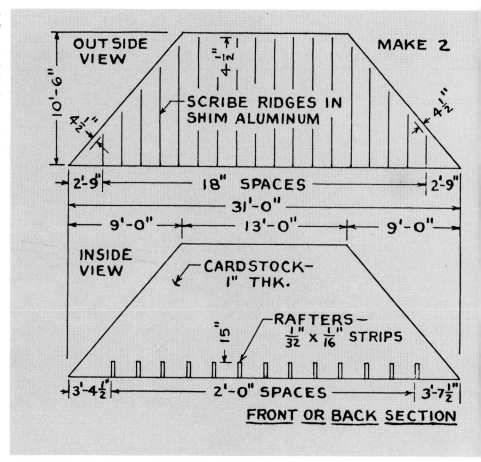

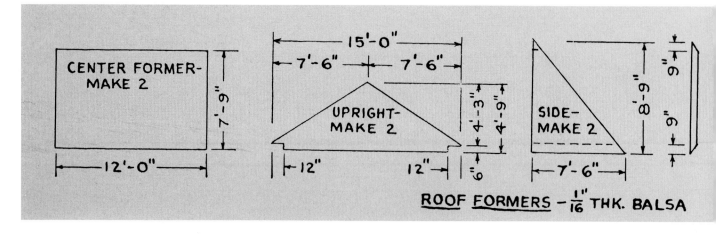

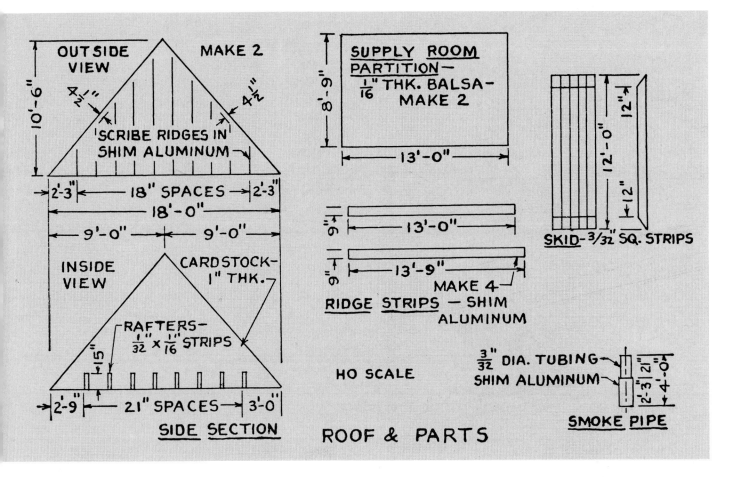

OUTSIDE VIEW — MAKE 2

10'-6"

$\frac{1}{2}$" x $\frac{1}{2}$"

4$\frac{1}{2}$"

SCRIBE RIDGES IN SHIM ALUMINUM

2'-3"   18" SPACES   2'-3"

18'-0"

9'-0"   9'-0"

INSIDE VIEW

CARDSTOCK— $\frac{1}{32}$" THK.

RAFTERS— $\frac{1}{32}$" x $\frac{1}{16}$" STRIPS

15"

2'-9"   21" SPACES   3'-0"

SIDE SECTION

SUPPLY ROOM PARTITION— $\frac{1}{16}$" THK. BALSA— MAKE 2

9'-8"

13'-0"

9"   13'-0"

9"   13'-9"

MAKE 4

RIDGE STRIPS — SHIM ALUMINUM

HO SCALE

ROOF & PARTS

SKID— $\frac{3}{32}$" SQ. STRIPS

12"

12'-0"

12"

$\frac{3}{32}$" DIA. TUBING

SHIM ALUMINUM

2'-3"   4'-0"

SMOKE PIPE

with a pencil. Be careful not to cut yourself on the sharp edges.

Draw the four roof sections on the metal. Put several thicknesses of paper on a drawing board or table and place the aluminum on the paper. Scribe the ridges representing joints between sheets of tin roofing. The ridges stop about 4½" from the upper edges of the sections where the joints are supposedly bent down for the application of peak strips.

Cut out the metal parts. Then make four card stock parts the same sizes. On the inside of the card, mark the locations of the rafters. Cement metal and cardboard together.

Cut 46 rafters 15" long from ⅟32" x ⅟16" stripwood. Cement them, on edge,

to the inside of the roof. You will have four rafters left. Save them for the corners at assembly. Paint the rafters and the space between them.

Make one ridge strip 9" x 13'-0" long, and four strips 9" x 13'-9" long. Cut these strips from shim aluminum.

The smoke pipe is a piece of ¾2" tubing 4'-0" long. Wrap and cement a strip of shim metal 2'-3" wide around the bottom of the tube.

The final piece is a skid resembling the middle of a timber grade crossing. The prototype has just one located in front of the left-hand door. You may want to make two. Cement five ¾2"-square strips together and bevel the ends. See drawing above.

Before proceeding to assembly,

compare the walls and roof sections. Where a rafter will touch a cap, cut off the cap 7½" down from the top of the wall.

Assembly

To put the building together, start with the base and floor and the back wall. The ⅟16" bracing fits on top of the floor. The inside of the wall below this strip fits against the edge of the floor, while the bottom edge of the wall rests on top of the piles. Cement the wall and hold it temporarily with pins, checking to see that wall and floor form a right angle.

Add the front wall, fitting it against the edge of the floor and the top section of the base. Place the side walls outside the front and back walls with their bottom bracing against the floor. Slip the two supply-room partitions between the front and back walls. These go between the middle vertical braces as shown on page 57.

See the back view and section A-A, page 57, for locations of roof formers. First, place the two upright formers, spacing them 7'-6" from each side of the building. Be sure they are vertical. Add the two rectangular center formers inside the uprights. Place two side formers at either end and cement them to the uprights and the tops of the walls. Cement the end formers between the side formers.

When the cement on the formers

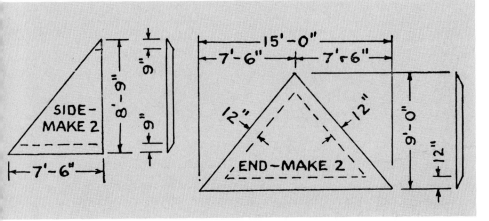

SIDE— MAKE 2

8'-9"

9"   9"

7'-6"

15'-0"

7'-6"   7'-6"

12"   12"

END—MAKE 2

9'-0"

12"

has dried, lay the roof. Coat formers and roof sections with cement. Press the sections in place with the false rafters against the walls. Cement a ridge strip, for 4½" of its width, along each joint. After the cement is dry, bend the strip along the center and cement it to the other side of the joint.

About 14'-0" from the right side of the roof, and 2'-6" from the peak, punch a hole and insert the smoke pipe. Put a rafter at each corner of the building.

If you have painted during construction, your tool house is complete. To age the building, give the roof a coat of thin gray, making it darker at the eaves. Weather the walls with thin washes of brown and black, or brush on powdered brown chalk or pastels for authentic dirt.

The top of the base should be covered with cinders, but you may not want to do this until the tool house is blended with the scenery on your layout. Paint the base dark gray; coat it with a slow-drying glue and sprinkle it with cinders. You can get a good supply of cinders by crushing and sifting some black clinkers.

NORTHEASTERN SCRIBED
SHEATHING—$\frac{1}{32}$" THK.—$\frac{1}{16}$"
SPACING.

SHUTTER—MAKE 6

BILL OF MATERIALS
(HO scale)

Base:	$\frac{1}{16}$" plywood, 4" x 5"; $\frac{1}{8}$" plywood, 5" x 6".
Floor:	$\frac{1}{32}$" balsa, 3" x 4½".
Floor, partitions and formers:	$\frac{1}{16}$" balsa, 3" x 10½".
Walls:	Northeastern capped siding, $\frac{1}{16}$" with $\frac{1}{8}$" spacing, 3½" x 6".
Doors, shutters:	Northeastern scribed sheathing, $\frac{1}{32}$" with $\frac{1}{16}$" spacing, 2½" x 3½".
Hinges:	Cloth, ½" x ¾".
Latches:	3 spikes, 3 pins.
Bracing:	$\frac{1}{16}$"-square strip-wood, 28".
Trim, rafters:	$\frac{1}{32}$" x $\frac{1}{16}$" stripwood, 41".
Roof:	Shim aluminum, 1½" x 11"; card stock, 1½" x 11".
Smoke pipe:	$\frac{3}{32}$" tubing, $\frac{9}{16}$" length.
HO rail:	14".

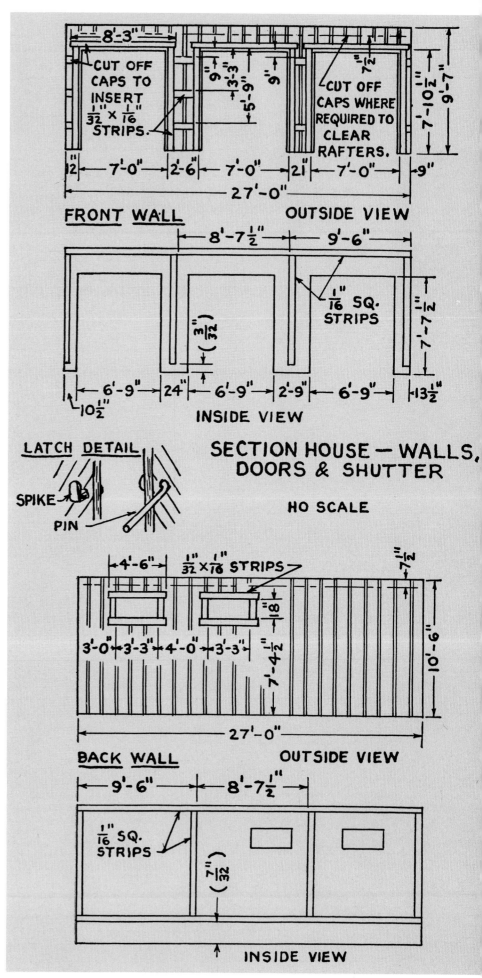

SECTION HOUSE — WALLS, DOORS & SHUTTER

HO SCALE

LATCH DETAIL

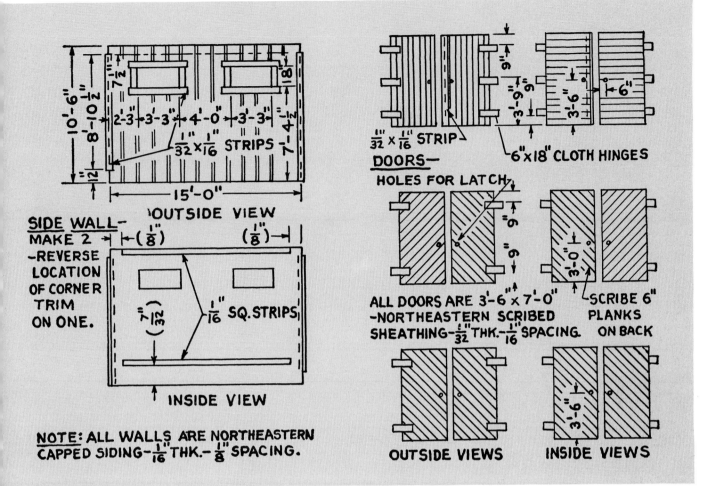

SIDE WALL—
MAKE 2
—REVERSE
LOCATION
OF CORNER
TRIM
ON ONE.

OUTSIDE VIEW

$\frac{1}{32} \times \frac{1}{16}$ STRIPS

$\frac{1}{16}$ SQ. STRIPS

INSIDE VIEW

NOTE: ALL WALLS ARE NORTHEASTERN CAPPED SIDING—$\frac{1}{16}$" THK.—$\frac{1}{8}$" SPACING.

$\frac{1}{32} \times \frac{1}{16}$ STRIP

6"x18" CLOTH HINGES

DOORS—
HOLES FOR LATCH

ALL DOORS ARE 3'-6" x 7'-0"
—NORTHEASTERN SCRIBED
SHEATHING—$\frac{1}{32}$" THK.—$\frac{1}{16}$" SPACING.

SCRIBE 6"
PLANKS
ON BACK

OUTSIDE VIEWS

INSIDE VIEWS

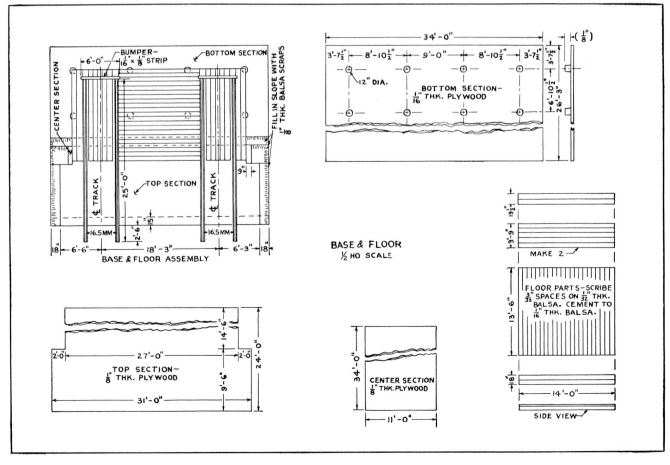

BUMPER—
$\frac{1}{16}$" x $\frac{1}{8}$" STRIP

BOTTOM SECTION

CENTER SECTION

FILL IN SLOPE WITH $\frac{1}{8}$" THK. BALSA SCRAPS

TOP SECTION

$\mathbb{C}$ TRACK

16.5MM

16.5MM

BASE & FLOOR ASSEMBLY

BOTTOM SECTION—
$\frac{1}{16}$" THK. PLYWOOD

12" DIA.

BASE & FLOOR
$\frac{1}{2}$ HO SCALE

MAKE 2

FLOOR PARTS—SCRIBE $\frac{3}{32}$" SPACES ON $\frac{1}{32}$" THK. BALSA. CEMENT TO $\frac{1}{16}$" THK. BALSA.

SIDE VIEW

TOP SECTION—
$\frac{1}{8}$" THK. PLYWOOD

CENTER SECTION
$\frac{1}{8}$" THK. PLYWOOD

Chas. L. Franck.

PUT A ROOF OVER THEIR HEADS

Trackworkers' dwelling

BY JOE WILHELM

THE men who maintain the track on a railroad must never be too far from their charge. Therefore, every railroad's right of way is lined with little villages of gandy dancers' homes. They form quite an important part of the wayside scenery on prototype roads and are something that is very much neglected on model railroads. This structure is copied from a double dwelling on the Texas & Pacific RR. Actually you should build several like

it to place in a row along part of your right of way. Add a few fences, some sort of outhouses, and car garages nearby to complete the picture.

Fig. 1 shows the simple construction of this building. There are no ins and outs of the walls to complicate things. I used heavy file cardboard for my house. Take the measurements from the templates in Fig. 2 and cut out the sides and ends. Then mark the windows and doors and cut them out.

Next, put in the windows and their framing. I drew the framing and mullions on sheet acetate with airplane dope in a ruling pen. Glue the windows in position on the inside of the cardboard walls. Cut the battens from cardboard or wood and glue them on the outside as per the drawings. When all this is complete, the four main parts of the building may be assembled, but you will probably want to paint them before doing so. My model

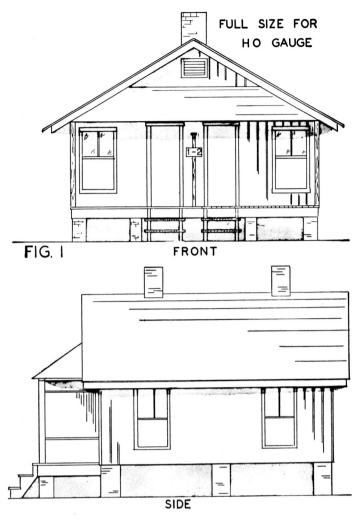

FULL SIZE FOR
HO GAUGE

FIG. 1   FRONT

SIDE

To use these plans and templates for any gauge, measure them with the HO scale rule, then measure your work with the proper rule for your own gauge.

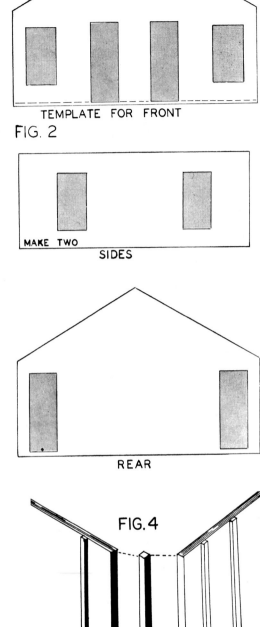

TEMPLATE FOR FRONT

FIG. 2

MAKE TWO

SIDES

REAR

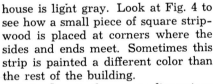

PORCH
FLOOR

FIG. 3

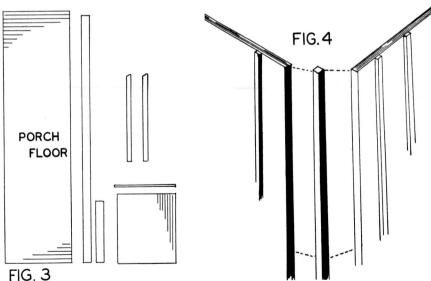

FIG. 4

house is light gray. Look at Fig. 4 to see how a small piece of square stripwood is placed at corners where the sides and ends meet. Sometimes this strip is painted a different color than the rest of the building.

Cut a floor to the proper dimensions of the building; check it against the rectangular space inside the sides and ends. This should be made of very heavy cardboard or wood. Brace all the inside edges with ⅛"-square balsa wood. This will make the structure quite strong.

Next, cut out the roof and glue it in position. Use file card for this and cut it in two pieces. Cut strips of thin paper and glue them on to simulate tar paper. Paint the roof flat black.

Cut the porch by using the templates in Fig. 3. I started to give templates for the porch roof, but you'll find it easier to fit this by trial and error, for the smallest variation in dimensions will throw out any measurements I might give. Just make it in three pieces and trim and fit until it looks right. Make the steps from sheet balsa of the proper thickness.

The footings for the house are made from a strip of square balsa. Paint these a flat brick red and draw on the mortar lines with white paint or ink. Place them around the edges as shown and put a few in the middle of the house to strengthen it. The chimney is made the same way and the notch where it fits on the top of the roof should be cut very carefully.

Notice that there is a wooden separation between the two doors on the porch. This is to insure a little privacy for the respective families. Cut it from cardboard or balsa wood.

Lineside Railroad Structures   63

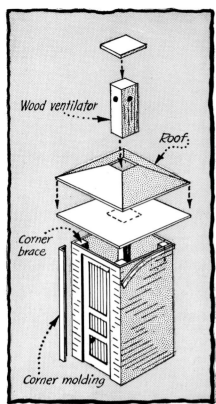

Wood ventilator

Roof

Corner brace

Corner molding

Telephone shack

TELEPHONE shacks are located at frequent intervals along the right of way for use of crews in contacting the train dispatcher. They are very much in evidence on prototype roads.

The phone shack shown here can be built from cardboard, wood or a combination of both. It will be just as easy to make three or four at the same time.

If cardboard sides are used, cut them from one folded piece. Scribe it as shown to represent sheathing; this can be done with a 6H round-pointed draftsman's pencil. If wood is used for the sides, the grain should be horizontal to make scribing easier. The door can be scribed as an integral part of one of the walls, or it can be a separate piece behind the door opening.

Moldings are narrow paper strips. Five pieces — four roof segments and the base — make up the roof. Either wood or thin card can be used and the segments can be made from one piece. The ventilator shaft can be wood.

If you want to locate the shack over a fill, support it with 12 x 12 timbers. For O gauge these will be ¼" square; for S gauge ³⁄₁₆"; and for HO, ⅛".

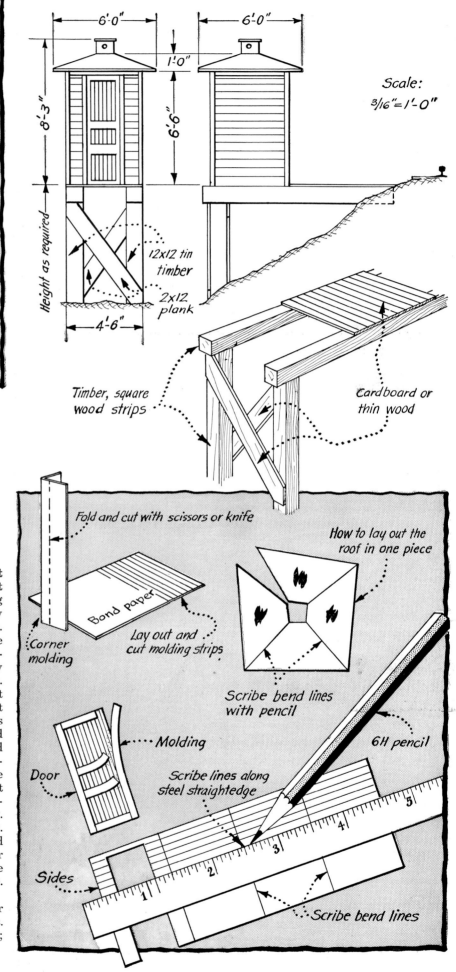

Scale:
3/16" = 1'-0"

12x12 tin timber

2x12 plank

Timber, square wood strips

Cardboard or thin wood

Fold and cut with scissors or knife

How to lay out the roof in one piece

Corner molding

Bond paper

Lay out and cut molding strips

Scribe bend lines with pencil

Molding

Door

Scribe lines along steel straightedge

6H pencil

Sides

Scribe bend lines

Easy-to-make rail racks

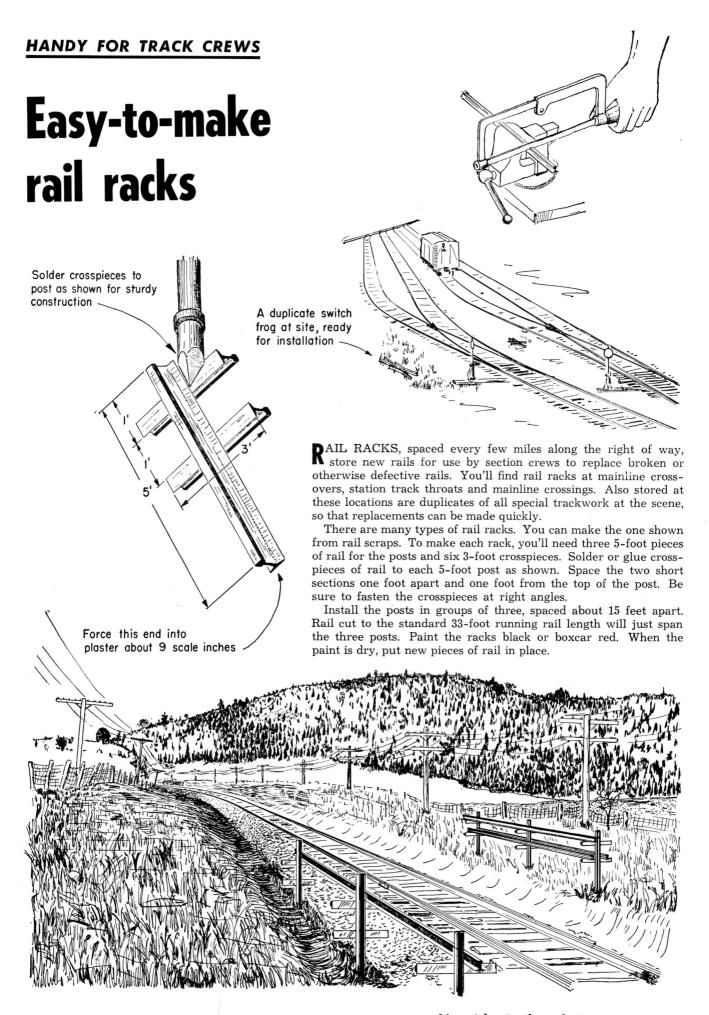

Solder crosspieces to post as shown for sturdy construction

A duplicate switch frog at site, ready for installation

Force this end into plaster about 9 scale inches

RAIL RACKS, spaced every few miles along the right of way, store new rails for use by section crews to replace broken or otherwise defective rails. You'll find rail racks at mainline crossovers, station track throats and mainline crossings. Also stored at these locations are duplicates of all special trackwork at the scene, so that replacements can be made quickly.

There are many types of rail racks. You can make the one shown from rail scraps. To make each rack, you'll need three 5-foot pieces of rail for the posts and six 3-foot crosspieces. Solder or glue crosspieces of rail to each 5-foot post as shown. Space the two short sections one foot apart and one foot from the top of the post. Be sure to fasten the crosspieces at right angles.

Install the posts in groups of three, spaced about 15 feet apart. Rail cut to the standard 33-foot running rail length will just span the three posts. Paint the racks black or boxcar red. When the paint is dry, put new pieces of rail in place.

An easily made relay shed
for your pike

BY L. M. OPIE

HERE is a simple lineside structure to dress up your passing sidings and take away the bare look of remote-controlled turnouts. The prototype for this model is a mass-produced precast concrete structure used either for housing signal relays or as a telephone booth. The signal data in the *Model Railroader Cyclopedia* shows a relay shed used on the Milwaukee Road, and I used it to obtain dimensions for my model.

As you can see in the photos, the model consists simply of a wooden dowel for the body of the shed (the one I used came from the rung of a chair); a disc of wood for the footing; another coned disc for the roof; and four strips of bond paper for trim and door hinges. The plans are for HO, but you can use the scale rules in this book to build in O or S gauge.

To make the footing, use a disc of balsa a scale 4'-9" in diameter and 6"

thick. You need a piece of dowel 4'-6" in diameter and 9 feet long for the body. Make the doorway as follows:

Scribe a line the length of the dowel and two lines parallel to the ends 6" from the bottom and 1 foot from the top, as shown in the diagram. Drop another vertical to make the door 2'-6" wide. Use a jeweler's hacksaw or a Zona saw to make two cuts along the horizontal lines, just deep enough to reach the vertical lines. Cut the

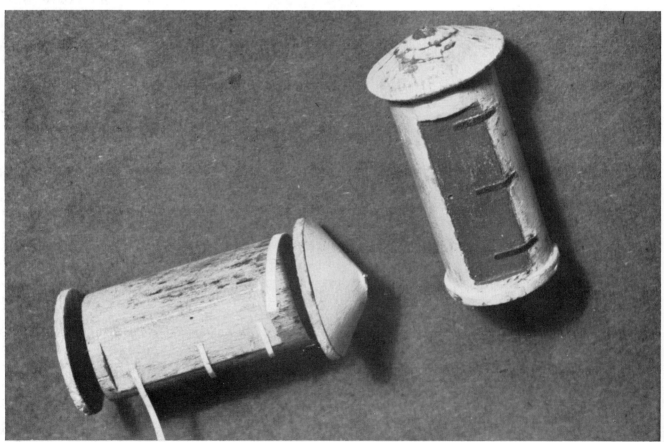

Both photos, Lionel E. Bates.

Three pieces of wood and paper trim make this relay shed, yet it looks like the real thing when painted up. The wooden dowel is the main structure piece, and strips of paper are used to make door hinges and trim under the roof.

excess wood away with an X-acto knife or chisel, and finish off with a fine file.

For the roof you need a disc of balsa 5'-3" in diameter and 2 feet thick. Cement this to the body and then slope the sides up to a cone with a file. Finish off with fine sandpaper.

To trim the shed, cement a strip of bond paper around the body, butted against the underside of the roof. Make the hinges of the door from strips of bond paper 2 feet long and 2" wide. If you like, impress bolts in them with a scriber. Use a lill head for a doorknob.

Paint the door of your relay shed boxcar red, and the door hinges black. The body of the shed should be an off-white to represent weathered concrete. Because the prototype sheds are exposed to the elements and get very little maintenance, the dirtier and more rundown your model shed looks, the more true to prototype it will be.

If you want to build several relay sheds, make a simple latex mold and you will be able to produce sheds in quantity from plaster. If the shed is to be used as a telephone booth, stick a pin in the crown of the roof and bend the end of it in an inverted U shape. With a dab of cement, fasten a piece of thread to the pin and run it to the nearest telephone pole.

The doorway of the relay shed has the most detail, but even that won't take very long to make. An X-acto knife and a fine file are all you need for it.

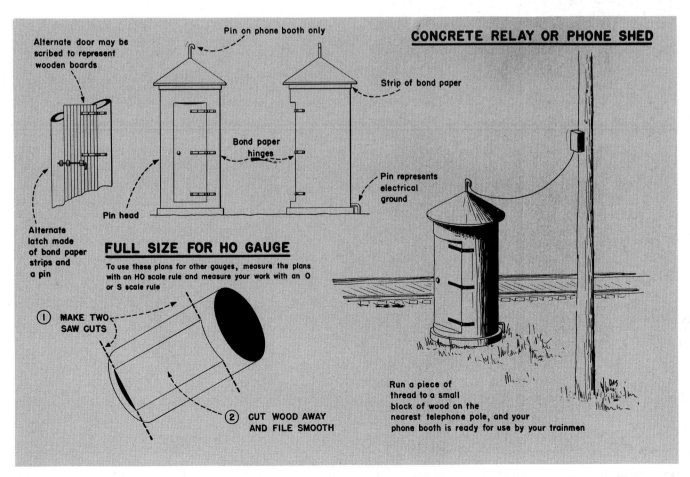

Alternate door may be scribed to represent wooden boards

Pin on phone booth only

CONCRETE RELAY OR PHONE SHED

Strip of bond paper

Bond paper hinges

Pin represents electrical ground

Alternate latch made of bond paper strips and a pin

Pin head

FULL SIZE FOR HO GAUGE

To use these plans for other gauges, measure the plans with an HO scale rule and measure your work with an O or S scale rule

① MAKE TWO SAW CUTS

② CUT WOOD AWAY AND FILE SMOOTH

Run a piece of thread to a small block of wood on the nearest telephone pole, and your phone booth is ready for use by your trainmen

Build a gateman's tower

BY RICHARD HOUGHTON

THE gateman watches the approach of the streamliner from his tower at the street crossing, then starts the mechanism that lowers the gates. Here it comes, smoke streaming along its back. Drivers flash. The tower trembles. The gateman is two stories up and only 6 feet from the nearest

rail. Walls and floor shake and windows rattle as the train roars past.

Almost every railroad in the nation uses one or more of these towers at highway crossings on its lines. They are eye-catchers for lovers of typical railroad architecture. However, a modeler who wants to build one will find that no architectural plans exist. A few measurements and photographs made possible the drawings of the SP tower shown on these pages.

The tower is a simple structure to build. Model trainmen who want to make it in an easy way can (1) draw the various window and door frames and other trim in ink on four cardboard walls; (2) cut out the openings and behind them cement plastic windows on which the mullions have been drawn or painted; (3) install a porch, stairway, railings, roof and chimney; (4) apply paint; and the job's done. It's not a model-in-a-minute, but it might be finished in an evening. However, if you want to include all the detail which appears in the photo of the SP tower, the following procedure is recommended.

The plans given here are in HO scale, so if you want them in S or O scale, simply measure the distance on the correct rule which appears on page 2 or 3. This will save you the tedious work of drawing up plans to another scale.

Select a fairly thin, hard cardboard

for your surfacing material. You will use this, four-ply thick, to surface the core of your building, so determine how thick four layers will be and then shrink the core dimensions to suit.

The core is a solid block of wood, drilled and cut as shown in photo A. Start with a block much larger than you'll need. Otherwise it will split when you drill the main vertical hole which lets light up into the building from a light bulb concealed below. Cut the core down to size and saw out ample holes for window openings. Photo A also shows how the heavy cardboard porch floor is installed, for strength, right through the building, with a hole in the "room" floor, of course, to let the light through.

Lay a piece of carbon paper on your thin cardboard, and your drawings on top of that. You can transfer the lines of the drawings to the cardboard as needed, using a straightedge and a sharp pointed tool. Perhaps a nail will do.

The first layer of cardboard will cover the four sides of the core. The window and door openings are determined by the "nail and carbon paper" method, and the width of the cardboard is determined by the width of the core. Photo B shows how it is held with rubber bands until the cement sets.

The second layer of cardboard is cut with oversize openings. Cement clear

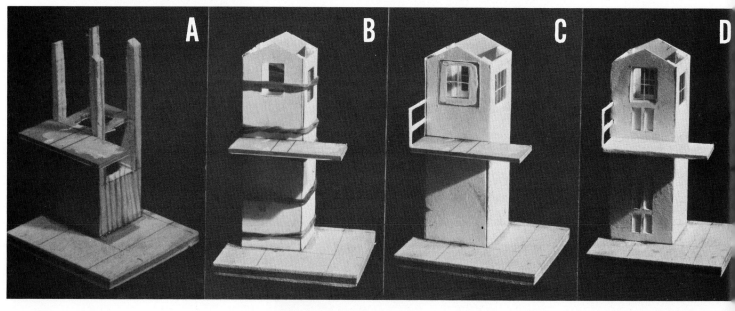

plastic windows into these openings. If possible, the windows should be the same thickness as the cardboard. Paint mullions and sash on the sheet of plastic, as shown in photo C. Now the first part of the railing can be installed. The post and two rails can be cut from the same piece of cardboard which covers that side of the building. A wood post can be cemented against the cardboard post to reinforce it.

The third layer of cardboard has window and door glass openings and door panels, all cut to the exact size of the drawings, as seen in photo D.

Detailed cutting is involved in the fourth layer, as shown in photo E. This lamination will bring the building to its full size. Edges should be beveled for neat corners. The cutting shown in the photo was done with a sharp razor blade. Do not attempt to cut clear through the cardboard with one stroke. Take it easy. Repeat strokes until the razor cuts through — there will be less danger of the blade wandering. A blade broken into a point will cut into the right-angled corners satisfactorily.

A nice touch is to add sloping window sills and pinheads for doorknobs, as in photo F, which also shows the cardboard stairway, the posts set into the holes in the base, and the roof reinforced with a small angle of wood.

If you cement shingle strips to the roof, use rubber cement to avoid warping. Drill through the roof and insert the chimney, which can be made of stiff paper. Cement on false rafters. Railings are cardboard, reinforced with wood where advisable.

Most of the building is painted a diluted yellow ochre. Shaded parts of the drawing are a light tan or burnt sienna. The roof is a light green, and the chimney black.

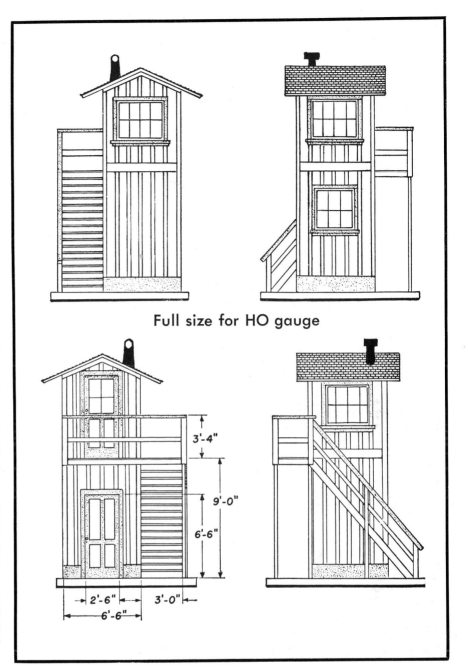

Full size for HO gauge

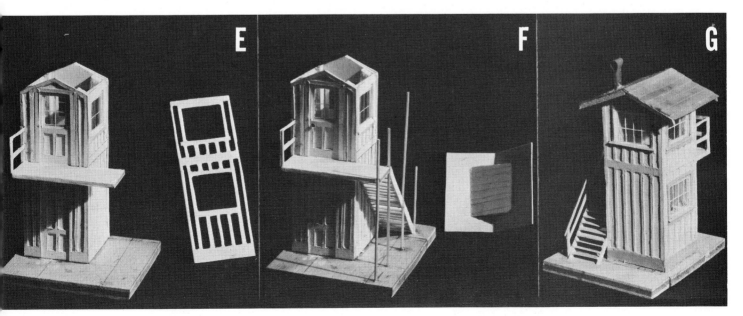

A HETEROGENEOUS CONGLOMERATION

OF THISA AND THATA

Besides being easy to make, these accessories are easy to look at when you put them on the right of way. They give the intersection a busy look.

RAILROAD HASH

BY EUGENE LE DOUX

Photos by the author

HOW often have you heard people say, "It's the little things that count"? That's a phrase that could apply to many projects, but it's especially appropriate for model railroading. Instead of dealing with just one structure in this article, I thought it would be a good idea to describe several "little things."

I selected a group of five railroad accessories which I think most of you can use. The only building material you will need is cardboard, scribed wood, clapboard siding, sandpaper, glue, paint, India ink and a few other miscellaneous materials. Line those things up and you're all set.

The first item on the list is a telephone cable reel. Second is a lineman's shack. You'll find dozens of these small buildings along any railroad's right of way. The third item is something no railroad should be without — crossing gates. They could even be made to work manually or electrically with a little extra effort. To

go along with the crossing gates I've included a watchman's shanty. Last but not least there's a crossing signal which all safety-conscious railroads feature at intersections with a highway.

Telephone Cable Reel

As you can see in the photo on page 73, the foundation for the cable reel is an old Scotch-tape spool. These spools come in various sizes so you should be able to obtain one which fits the approximate dimensions for your gauge. If for any reason such a spool is unavailable, substitutes can be made from a thread spool, a mailing tube, a paper towel roll or a piece of wood dowel. The foundation is relatively unimportant except that it provides the required shape.

The construction is shown in Fig. 1. Glue strips of thin scribed wood around the spool you select. If you cut a long, narrow strip it may crack or even break when you wrap it around the spool. You can disregard that be-

cause the glue will hold it down at the break and elsewhere. While the glue is still wet, tie two bands of black thread or wire tightly around the spool. Next, cut two card discs with small holes in the center. Scribe and then draw boards on these discs with India ink. When you have that done, glue them to the sides of the spool.

All that remains now are the finishing touches. Add a few sign boards similar to those shown on the plans. Magazines, desk calendars and calling cards provide an unlimited source of signboard material. You will seldom see these telephone cable reels painted, but they often have a weathered appearance. This can be obtained by brushing used lacquer thinner over the surface to be treated. The faint lettering on the side around the edge can be drawn on with ordinary lead pencil. By making the letters barely visible it won't matter if they are slightly imperfect.

When you have made a few of these

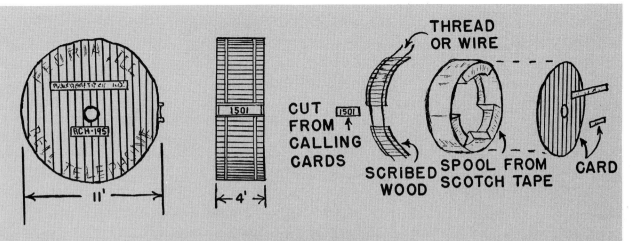

THREAD OR WIRE

CUT FROM CALLING CARDS

1501

SCRIBED WOOD

SPOOL FROM SCOTCH TAPE

CARD

1501

RCH·195

11'

4'

Fig. 1   Telephone Cable Reels

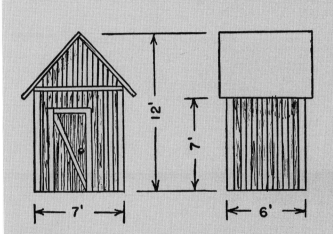

FINE SANDPAPER

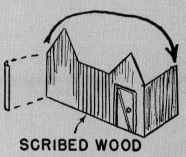

SCRIBED WOOD

12'

7'

7'

6'

Fig. 2   Lineman's Shack

FULL SIZE FOR HO GAUGE

To use these plans for O or S gauge, use the proper scale rule (pages 33 and 34) to transfer the measurements to your work.

GLUE STRIPS TOGETHER

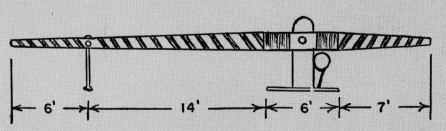

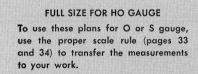

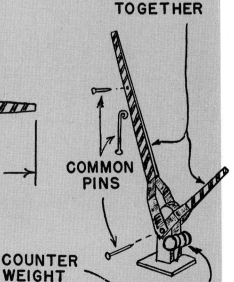

6'   14'   6'   7'

COMMON PINS

COUNTER WEIGHT

Fig. 3   Crossing Gates

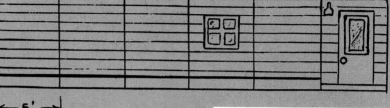

Watchman's Shanty

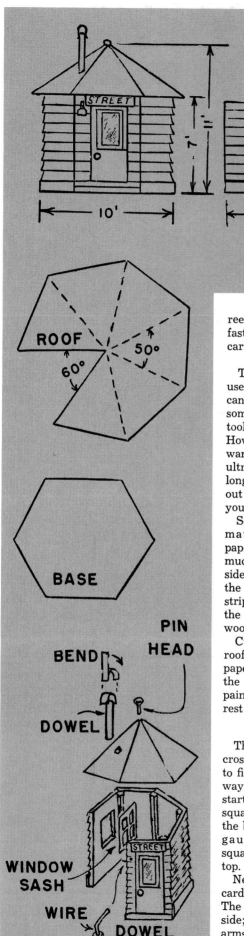

Fig. 4

reels, place them along a highway or fasten them down to an empty flat car.

Lineman's Shack

The plans for this building can be used to make other buildings which can serve different purposes. In fact, some may think this one resembles a tool shed more than a lineman's shack. However, you can decide what you want to do with it. Construction is ultra-simple and shouldn't take very long. Several shacks could be turned out in an evening and put to use on your pike the same night.

Scribed wood is the most important material required, also fine sandpaper and cardboard. You'll find it much easier to cut the scribed wood sides out in one piece, then snap it at the corners and glue in reinforcing strips of wood. The framework around the door can be either card or stripwood. Fig. 2 gives the dimensions.

Cut out a piece of card to fit the roof and glue it to a sheet of fine sandpaper of the same dimensions. Glue the roof to the shack and be sure to paint the sandpaper black. Paint the rest of the shed and you're finished.

Crossing Gates

The dimensions for the arms of the crossing gates may have to be changed to fit the width of your road or highway. Check that detail before you start. After that, cut a 6-scale-foot-square base from a piece of card. To the base glue a post (½" square for O gauge, ¼" square for HO and ⅜" square for S gauge) rounded at the top.

Next, cut two pairs of identical card strips for the arms of each gate. The short pair is for the pedestrian side; the other is for the cars. The arms should be long enough so they will overlap where they are attached to the post with pins. Drill a hole be-

fore inserting the pins. This will allow the arms to be raised and lowered. Attach a leg support 6 scale feet from the end of the arm as shown in Fig. 3.

Paint diagonal stripes of white and black on both sides of the arms. An easy way to do this is to paint the entire arm white. Then draw the black stripes on with a pen and India ink. Paint the post brown or black and the base cement-gray. You can omit the counterweight if you wish and glue the base to "terra firma" instead. The gates are top-heavy and so they must be fastened or weighted down in some manner. The advantage of a weight is that the gates can be moved to some other location.

Crossing Signal

Next on the agenda is a perfect mate for the crossing gates: a crossing signal. This type is seen throughout the country and is becoming a common sight at every railroad crossing. The materials required are: stripwood (¼" square for O gauge, ⅛" square for HO and ³⁄₁₆" square for S gauge), thin card stock and two washers.

Select the size of stripwood for your gauge and cut a piece 15 scale feet long. Attach it to a cardboard base with a pin or nail. Drill a hole for the pin up through the center of the post. (See Fig. 5.) Make the signboards from thin card stock. Paint them with several coats of white and let them dry thoroughly. With a fine pen point and India ink, carefully print "Railroad Crossing" on one pair. If you'd rather, you can type the sign on white card, but use capital letters instead of lower case ones. Take the other signboard which was painted white and cover it completely with India ink. Using a pen point, carefully print the number of tracks at the crossing. The pen point should neatly scrape off the India ink, revealing the white paint underneath. That way you have white letters on a black background.

Get the signal lights from your collection of washers. Cut a shield for

Here's a close-up of the author's railroad hash. You can see where the telephone cable reel comes from.

the lights as shown in Fig. 5 and glue the washers (lights, I should say) to a crossarm. The entire signal should be painted white except the lights, which I painted black. I believe they should be black so that there is a color contrast when the lights are flashing.

Although I am referring to the prototype, you could very easily put grain-o-wheat bulbs in the signal and hook them to a flasher unit. Couldn't you just see a sleek, shiny passenger train whiz by with the signals flashing their red warning to the motorists? When you're installing the signal alongside the track, simply drill a hole where it is to be placed and insert it there.

Watchman's Shanty

It seems that crossing accessories are getting priority here, so while we're at it why not construct a watchman's shanty? You see one at nearly every other highway grade crossing, and more often at busy crossings near the cities and suburbs. Because they are so common, you'll need at least one for your railroad.

The only different material required for this structure is clapboard siding. This should be available in basswood sheets at your hobby shop. If for any reason it's not, you can make your own by gluing cardboard strips which overlap each other to a piece of wood sheet or heavy card stock. If you plan to use the commercial siding, cut out each side individually. Otherwise cut one piece of card the full dimension of the building, bend it at the corners and glue the strips of thin card to this foundation. The plans (see Fig. 4)

show how each side should look. I suggest cutting the base from heavy card or 1/16" to 1/8" wood sheet. This base will give you a solid foundation for the sides.

Incidentally, if you glue a strip of wood to each inside corner, this will brace the sides considerably. Make the window frames and the door and glue them to the corresponding position on the side. Put on the celluloid window material after painting the shanty.

Cut the roof from a piece of cardboard from which a "slice" or wedge has been removed. The roof's diameter should be a little more than the

diameter of your model. Other pertinent data is on the roof pattern.

Bend the roof where indicated by the dotted lines. The roof top and door knob are made from common pin heads. The street name I used was cut from an address card, but it could be obtained from a newspaper or magazine. Cut or drill a hole in the roof for the chimney, which is made from a piece of wood dowel. As far as painting is concerned, no particular color is associated with a watchman's shanty, so the choice is up to you.

That's the end of the line for the railroad hash.

NOTE: TO MAKE AN ORDINARY CROSSBUCK SIMPLY OMIT SIGNAL LIGHTS AND TRACK NUMBER BOARD.

RAIL ROAD CROSSING

2 TRACKS

6'

5'

3'

2'

5'

10'

RAIL ROAD CROSSING

2 TRACKS

BEND

DRILL & INSERT

Fig. 5   Crossing Signal

The cows at the right don't seem very cheerful as they observe proceedings at the meat warehouse across the tracks.

PART 5: INDUSTRIAL AND MISCELLANEOUS WAYSIDE STRUCTURES

Meat warehouse

BY EUGENE LE DOUX

Photos by the author

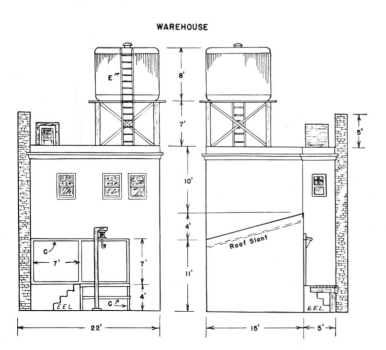

WAREHOUSE

REMEMBER the riddle that goes, "How can the brown cow eat green grass and give white milk?" I don't claim to know the answer to that one, but I do know that a cow gives beefsteak which can taste mighty good. Did you ever realize that very few of us would be able to enjoy a steak now and then if it weren't for the fast and inexpensive method of transporting perishable meat products by way of our country's railroads?

Perhaps you're wondering how I became interested in building this particular structure. One morning, when I was passing a Wilson & Co. warehouse, workmen were unloading sides of beef from a reefer located on a siding near by. It was quite a thrill to see big, juicy red sides of beef, sus-

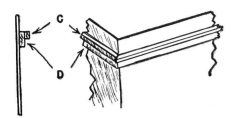

CORNICE ON WAREHOUSE

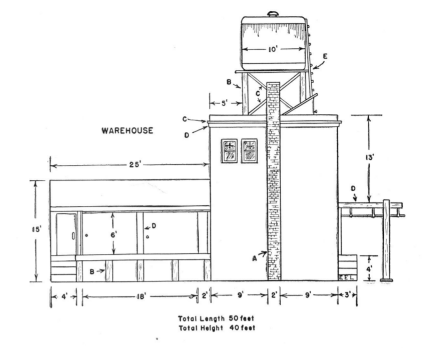

WAREHOUSE

Total Length 50 feet
Total Height 40 feet

pended by hooks, come sliding out of the reefer one after the other. They would roll over the tramway affair and disappear into the warehouse. Traffic on the street between the platform and the warehouse came to a halt during the operation, because of the low clearance of the tramway with a side of beef hanging from it. No vehicle could get underneath, unless it might be a low underslung sports car like a Jaguar or an MG.

While I watched the unloading procedure, I began to think of the modeling possibilities. Everything checked! It certainly was logical. What town, city, or hamlet doesn't have meat on its daily menu? It must be transported there some way and what way would be better than a railroad? Then, a meat warehouse could be put to use on small layouts as easily as on large ones. And it was attractive enough to spur on the modelmaking urge inside me, so here it is!

The structure is divided into two parts, the loading platform and the warehouse itself. The length of the platform can be changed to suit your needs. You can also alter the warehouse or build it exactly to the dimensions in the drawings. The plans are half and full size for HO, but for

the convenience of those working in other gauges I've included approximate prototype dimensions. I don't follow exact prototype dimensions very often because of space limitations on my layout.

For convenience I've also included a table of sizes for stripwood used in building the model. The sizes are for HO, S and O gauge. Besides stripwood, you'll need scribed wood, cardboard, celluloid, paper tape, wire and rail spikes.

The loading platform should more accurately be called an unloading platform, because it is here that the reefers discharge their load of meat. Cut out the floor from a piece of scribed wood and glue short posts on the bottom. Small bits of scribed wood

STRIPWOOD SIZES

	HO	S	O
A	$\frac{1}{4}$" SQ.	$\frac{3}{8}$" SQ.	$\frac{1}{2}$" SQ.
B	$\frac{1}{8}$" SQ.	$\frac{3}{16}$" SQ.	$\frac{1}{4}$" SQ.
C	$\frac{1}{16}$" SQ.	$\frac{3}{32}$" SQ.	$\frac{1}{8}$" SQ.
D	$\frac{1}{8}$" X $\frac{1}{16}$"	$\frac{3}{16}$" X $\frac{3}{32}$"	$\frac{1}{4}$" X $\frac{1}{8}$"
E	$\frac{1}{32}$" SQ.	$\frac{3}{64}$" SQ.	$\frac{1}{16}$" SQ.

glued to the underside framework will add to the appearance of the model but these are not absolutely necessary. The prototype had such boards along the side, with a few missing. Make the supporting posts for the roof from stripwood, as in Fig. 1 on page 77. On my model I used three, but if you decide to make the platform longer you'll need more posts.

Build the tramway under the roof using the photograph as a guide. Railroad spikes pushed into the wooden overhead beams hold up the wire rail of the tramway. Make the roof of cardboard with strips of paper tape laid lengthwise to simulate roofing paper. After the roof is glued to the three (or more) posts, the latter can be glued to the floor, but I believe a few small wood screws will hold the

Spikes pushed through the beams hold the wire rail of the tramway in place.

structure together more firmly. If you use the latter method, mark the positions where the posts meet the floor. Use a drill which is a size or two smaller than the screw you plan to use; drill the holes through the floor and into the posts so the wood won't split when you finally assemble the unit.

The length of the I-beam is optional. Simply make it long enough to suit your needs. The I-beam may be curved to allow the structure to occupy a narrow area. In this case use a metal bar for the I-beam instead of wood. The staples glued in each end of the I-beam allow you to lift it away when it's not in use, exactly like the prototype. Using railroad spikes and wire, you can make the tramway rail in the same manner as described for the loading platform. Fig. 2 will help to clarify these directions.

Make the wall for the highest part of the warehouse from one piece of card, scribed and bent at the corners.

Left end view

I-BEAM TO WAREHOUSE

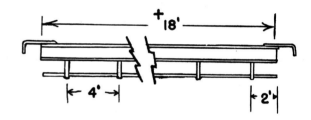

LOADING PLATFORM

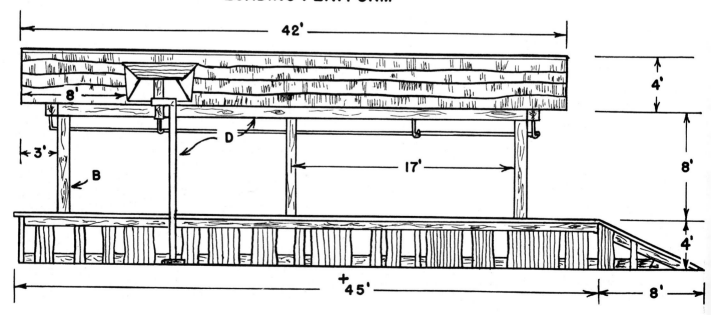

+(May be lengthened)

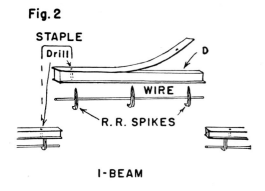

Fig. 2

STAPLE

Drill

D

WIRE

R.R. SPIKES

I-BEAM

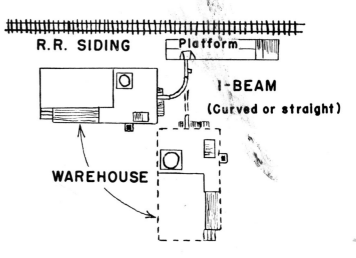

R.R. SIDING   Platform

I-BEAM
(Curved or straight)

WAREHOUSE

Make the low section the same way. These two sections are built independently and joined together later. Cut out and install the windows (see Fig. 3) and doors. Brace the corners of the building on the inside with type "A" stripwood. (See table of stripwood sizes.) Other sizes of stripwood used for platforms and framing can also be found in the table under the gauge in which you are building.

With India ink, draw the bricks on the chimney; wash them over with a thin mixture of paint. Either red or gray paint will do.

Build the water tower by wrapping scribed wood around a piece of tubing which has approximately the same dimensions. A washer or a rivet or the head of a bolt makes a realistic hatch for the top of the water tank. Set the tank on a scribed wood platform which is supported by braced stripwood posts. The I-beam leading into the warehouse is made exactly the same as the others.

I painted my model of the warehouse stucco gray, because it was quick, simple and looked good. However, you can easily put brick paper over the cardboard walls and still get a nice but different-looking type of warehouse. It may take a little longer to do, but I believe it would be worth the extra effort.

Also, you may want to put up a sign or some type of meat advertisement. Look through some of the women's magazines; you'll find dozens of meat ads that you can easily cut out and hang on the warehouse. Or you could type the name of the meat company on a piece of card and put that up.

Last but not least, you'll want your warehouse to come alive. Place a few workmen around the building, and a few trucks. Then, when your reefer rolls to a stop at the unloading platform, you'll be prepared to take care of the sides of beef as they come sliding out of the cars. When that's done, you can really enjoy that steak!

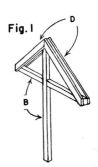

Fig. I

D

B

LOADING PLATFORM POSTS

Fig. 3

DRAW SASH WITH INDIA INK

CARD   CELLULOID

WINDOWS

Add action to the warehouse scene with workmen, automobiles and trucks set at logical places on platform and street.

Industrial and Miscellaneous Structures   77

GRAIN ELEVATOR

BY RAYMOND OVRESAT

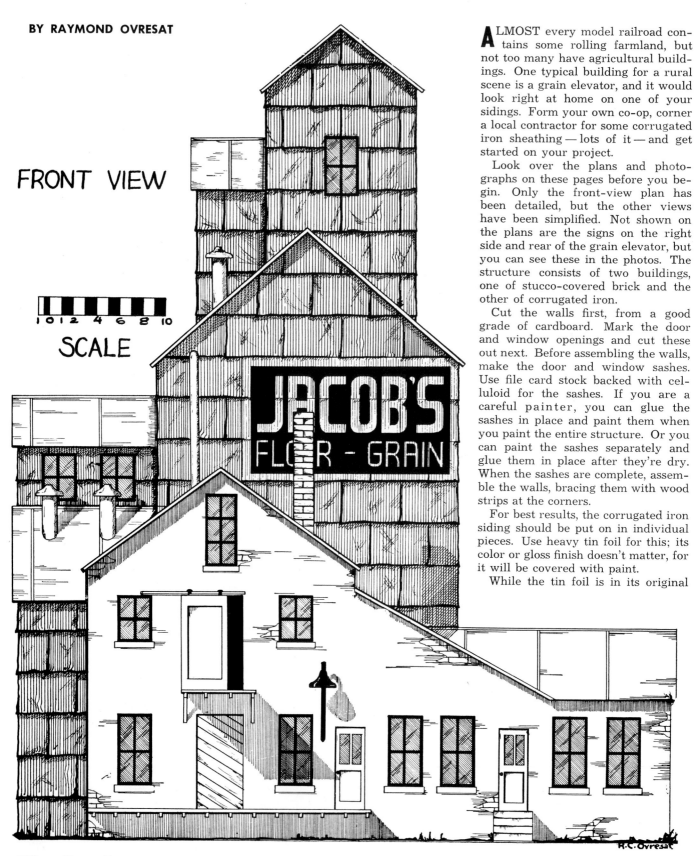

FRONT VIEW

SCALE

10 1 2 4 6 8 10

ALMOST every model railroad contains some rolling farmland, but not too many have agricultural buildings. One typical building for a rural scene is a grain elevator, and it would look right at home on one of your sidings. Form your own co-op, corner a local contractor for some corrugated iron sheathing — lots of it — and get started on your project.

Look over the plans and photographs on these pages before you begin. Only the front-view plan has been detailed, but the other views have been simplified. Not shown on the plans are the signs on the right side and rear of the grain elevator, but you can see these in the photos. The structure consists of two buildings, one of stucco-covered brick and the other of corrugated iron.

Cut the walls first, from a good grade of cardboard. Mark the door and window openings and cut these out next. Before assembling the walls, make the door and window sashes. Use file card stock backed with celluloid for the sashes. If you are a careful painter, you can glue the sashes in place and paint them when you paint the entire structure. Or you can paint the sashes separately and glue them in place after they're dry. When the sashes are complete, assemble the walls, bracing them with wood strips at the corners.

For best results, the corrugated iron siding should be put on in individual pieces. Use heavy tin foil for this; its color or gloss finish doesn't matter, for it will be covered with paint.

While the tin foil is in its original

sheet form, scribe the entire length of the sheet to represent the corrugation. Scribe it heavily, then cut the sheet into pieces the size of individual sheets of corrugated iron. Start at the bottom and glue the pieces in place. The righthand side of each piece should overlap the preceding piece slightly, and each row should overlap the row below it. When you get all the siding on, pry up some edges here and there to make the siding look warped and to give the sides even more relief.

The roofing comes next. Use the same type of cardboard for roofing that you used for the walls. Leave about a scale 6 inches to 1 foot overhang. Glue all the roofing in place. The type of roofing used for this building is the metal type made up of sheets. At the joints, one sheet is crimped over the edge of the other. You can represent these joints with small strips of wood, folded pieces of tin foil, or freight-car roof ribs. Whatever you use, don't worry about the color, because the whole roof will be painted aluminum later. Use tin-foil strips for the flashing in the valleys and the caps on the ridges of the roofs.

Add all the details before you do

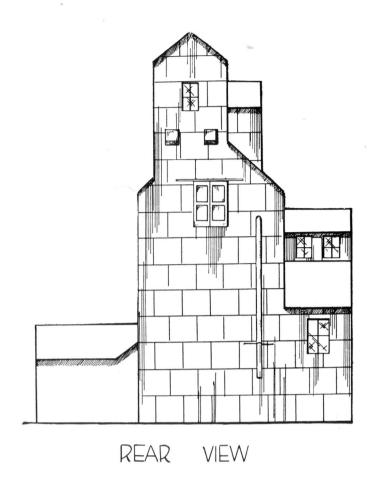

REAR VIEW

SCALE

1 0 1 2 4 6 8 10 12 14 16 18 20

RIGHT SIDE   LEFT SIDE

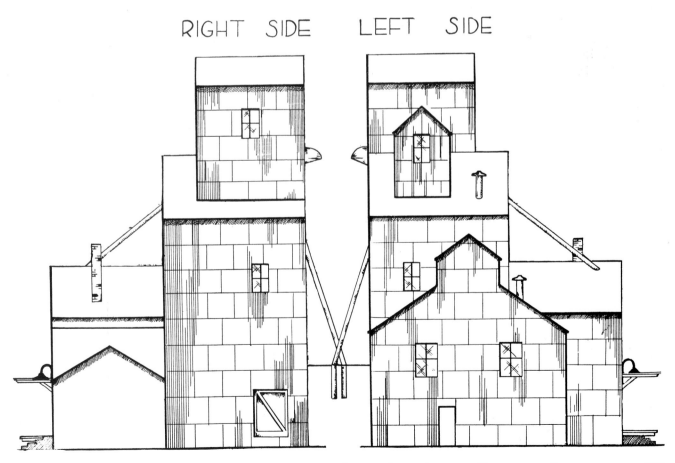

The signs look as if they haven't been painted for some time, but you'll have to paint them to get this effect.

Weathering a building of this sort gives it a more realistic appearance, and it's easier to do than you think.

any painting. Make the pipes for carrying grain from dowel rod. Ventilators on the roof are pieces of dowel topped with a trimmed collar button; or you might use a thumb tack or a small disk of heavy paper.

The two ventilators on the rear wall are carved from balsa wood. In modeling the doors you'll get a better effect if you leave some of them partially open. Freight doors on the front and back roll on a track of basswood. The rollers are blobs of black paint for HO gaugers.

The chimney is a strip of balsa wrapped in brick paper and smudged with candle smoke. The loading platforms are made from strips of filing cards supported by basswood stringers. They'll warp somewhat when painted and then have the proper weatherbeaten appearance.

The light is made from a collar button and a piece of wire. O gaugers could make the light a working one for a night-scene effect. The steps are tiers of balsa wood. Window sills on the stucco-covered portion are strips of balsa.

When these details are installed, you're ready to start painting. Start with the tinfoil siding. Use silver dope just thick enough to cover it. The roofing and door above the loading platform are also painted silver. This silver finish is just the first coat; you'll "weather" it by using tempera paint.

Tempera paint is actually thickened

water-color paint. Its advantages are that it dries quickly, leaves no gloss, and can easily be mixed and blended with other colors. It is *not* waterproof. When applied thickly, it has a tendency to chip and crack. Even so, it's ideal for most model work. In fact, its nonwaterproof characteristic becomes an advantage here.

Mix a little black tempera paint in with some brown for the "weathering" coat. With a large brush, go over every area you just painted silver. Work the paint well into every crevice and *cover the silver paint entirely*. After the tempera paint has dried, take a moistened piece of cotton or tissue and gently rub the areas just painted, removing most of the paint. Use a downward stroke. Don't rub so much that you remove *all* the paint, however.

The tempera coat will give the iron siding a rusty appearance. Allow the tempera paint to remain in places where rust would normally occur, especially where the sheets join and in the corrugations. The downward strokes will also create streaks of rust running down the sides.

If you manipulate the moistened cotton properly, you'll find you can vary the shades of the tempera paint and allow just enough on in places so that the apparent newness of the silver coat no longer exists. Practice this technique on a sheet of cardboard before tackling the siding itself.

The signs are painted directly on the sides, using the tempera paint. First give a coat of white to the entire area that the sign is to cover. After this has dried, block out the lettering and fill the areas between with black tempera paint. As I said before, tempera applied too thickly will tend to crack and chip. However, such behavior will help give the effect of age — so put it on thick. Dirty the lettering with dabs of thin gray paint. Rain often causes paint on signs to run, and this effect can be copied by applying thin streaks of diluted white tempera.

The stucco portion of the building is painted with a thick coat of gray tempera paint. Vary the shade in places and stipple the paint while applying it. Indicate uncovered areas of brick with touches of white and brown paint. Use a small brush to draw cracks in the stucco. The loading platforms are brown, shaded with black.

"Break" some of the windows in the freight elevator by cutting pieces out of the celluloid. Dirty others by covering them with black tempera, thinned considerably. In dry weather there always seems to be a thin layer of flour dust clinging to the sides of the grain elevator. This can be copied very nicely by rubbing talcum powder or ladies' face powder on the sides, then blowing off the excess. Don't use real flour; it isn't fine enough.

A complete mountain farm

Real railroads often pass a rural scene like this. From left to right: corn crib, barn, chicken house and home.

BY ROBERT E. GILBERT
Photos by the author

ONE of the pleasantest experiences of train riding is the view of rolling farmland that you get along the way. There's something very restful about just looking at the scenery as you go by. Don't forget your model passengers in that respect, or for that matter, visitors to your railroad. The latter are always impressed by scale scenery.

The mountain farm which I modeled in HO scale is just begging to be placed on your layout. It consists of a house, a barn, a spring house, a smokehouse, a corn crib, a chicken house and a hog house. The buildings are similar to actual structures that I've seen. For example, the barn is like one in Texas County, Mo., while the smokehouse resembles one in Washington County, Tenn.

This unit could well be the highlight of a small railroad, or it could make a very different-looking scene for a mountain on a large pike. Including barnyard, hog pen, pond and orchard, I have located the farm on hilly ground in a 24" square. The buildings themselves will fit in a 16" square of fairly level ground. For a smaller space, you could always eliminate some of the buildings. The house and barn alone will suggest a small farm if you haven't room for any more than that.

The plans are half and quarter size for HO gauge, while measurements in the text and plans are for HO. To build in O or S gauge, measure the half-size plans with your HO scale rule, double the figure, then measure

your work with the O gauge or the S gauge scale rule.

House

Begin construction of the house by taking dimensions from the plans and drawing the walls, which are in one piece, on Bristol board which is at least 1/32" thick. Cut out the window and door openings with a sharp blade. Cut out the walls and scribe them at the corners so they will bend easily.

Make three sets of window sash from index card stock. If you wish to have the windows raised, the lower half of the sash should also have a 1/32" strip across the bottom. Cement cellophane or acetate sheeting on the back of the sash sections.

Turn the walls over and cement the upper parts of the windows over the openings and then the lower, raising them if desired. Shades may be simulated by squares of brown paper, and curtains by strips of tissue paper.

The doors are sandwiches of index card with panels cut out in the top piece. Put glass or cellophane in the front door and thrust a small pin through each door for a knob. Attach the doors in either open or closed positions. Frame all door and window openings with 1/16" strips of thin Bristol or illustration board.

To give the walls the effect of boxed-and-stripped siding, prepare lengths of illustration board about 1/32" wide and cement them to the walls at intervals of from 3/32" to 5/32".

Make the floor of 3/32" sheet balsawood. Scribe lines not more than 1/8" apart for planking on the porches. Fold the walls around the floor; cement them and hold in place with pins until the cement dries.

Brace the walls on the inside with 1/8"-square wood strips, especially at the corners and across the peak of the roof. Outside, frame each corner with 1/16" strips of illustration board.

Make the porch frame beams from 1/16"-square strips. Whittle round, rough posts from stripwood, dowels or match sticks. Coat the top of each post with cement and hold it vertically against the beam until the cement has begun to set. When the completed frames have dried, put cement on the ends of the beams and the bottoms of the posts and set them in position on the porches.

Make the roof from Bristol board like that used for the walls. Scribe a line across the peak. Turn the roof over and scribe lines where it will bend at the porches. Attach the roof to the walls, holding it down with pins or rubber bands.

An inexpensive material for tin roofing can be made from empty toothpaste or shaving cream tubes. Cut the top and bottom from a tube, slit it open along one side, and wash it thoroughly, being careful not to injure yourself on sharp edges. Smooth the tube with some round object such as a pencil. Lightly sand both sides of the resulting flat sheet.

Cut out four sections of the metal, one to the dimensions of each slope

The front views of these small farm structures show a variety of detailing.

of the house roof. On the labeled side of the metal, draw lines ¼″ apart at the simulated joints between separate sheets of roofing. Take a block of wood — hard balsa will do — and cut a thin groove across it. Place a section of metal, shiny side down, on the block. Align the first line drawn on the metal with the groove in the wood; scribe along the line with the edge of a knife blade. This process will raise a sharp ridge in the metal. Continue scribing the lines until you have an imitation of a section of jointed tin roofing.

Smear the Bristol board roof of the house with cement and stick the metal to it. Fold ⅛″ strips of paper and cement them over the peak of the roof.

Make foundation stones from ¼″-square, ⅛″-thick balsa with rounded corners and edges. Thirteen are required. Make two ⅛″-square steps. Turn the building upside down and attach stones and steps. Place it upright on a flat surface and press down lightly to level the stones.

Whittle the chimneys from ¼″-thick balsa, cutting a depression in the top of each. You can either carve bricks into the sides of the chim-neys or cover them with brick paper.

Secure the kitchen chimney to the back wall while the house is still on a flat surface. Put the other chimney on the peak of the roof and the house is complete.

Barn

The barn consists of two sections of stalls joined by a central hayloft and roof. Make the walls of heavy Bristol board as you did for the house.

To represent rough board siding, cut out pieces of illustration board to the dimensions of the walls. It is easier to cover a small part at a time. With scissors, cut planks from 1/16″ to ⅛″ wide into the illustration board, letting the planks hang together by about 1/32″ of material at the top. Cover the walls with these sections of siding. Patch the walls with short lengths of board in a few places.

Cut the hayloft door and the stall doors from illustration board, scribing them to represent planks. Cement strips across several of the doors for framing. Cement all doors in place, some in an open position. Make hinges from index card stock and wooden latches from illustration board.

Build the ladder to the loft with 1/16″-square uprights and strips of illustration board spaced ⅛″ apart. Fold each stall section at the scored corners and cement it into a rectangle, holding the cemented edges together with pins. Run a 1/16″-square strip-wood sill along the walls inside. Brace them with ⅛″ strips.

Cut the loft floor from heavy Bristol board and fasten round beams across it. Put cement on two edges of the floor and the ends of the beams, and let it become tacky. Then line up the two stall sections and locate the loft floor over the driveway between them. When the cement has dried, strengthen the bond with ⅛″ braces across the peak of the roof.

Build the shed frame as you did the porch frames for the house, and attach it to the barn wall. Cut out the shed roof and cement it to the frame and wall. Make the main roof, scribe the joints and fasten it over the barn. The roof is covered and patched with several materials. For the wooden shingles, manufacture a number of ¼″ strips using scissors and index cards. To represent individual shingles, stack three or four strips and fringe the edges at intervals of about ⅛″ to a depth of about 3/16″.

Cover part of the center of the loft roof, the shed roof and the lean-to roofs with shingles. Leave part of one lean-to roof to be covered with tin. Beginning at the bottom edge of a roof, apply a strip of shingles and continue upward in overlapping rows 3/16″ part. Patch the shingles here and there with short planks.

Use fine black emery paper to make several strips of tar paper, and put these on the center of the loft roof overlapping the shingles. Patch one lean-to roof with tar paper.

Make tin roofing as described for the house and cover the remainder of the barn roof. Cut several pieces of metal about ¼″ x ½″; bend and cement them over the top of the roof in the middle.

Chicken House

Construction of the chicken house is very much like that of the barn on a smaller scale. Make the walls according to measurements taken from the plans; cover them with insulation board planking. Cement the door to the opening and put slats across the windows.

Cement the walls around a 1/16″ sheet balsa floor. Brace them inside. Add a plank for the chickens to walk up to the small door.

Cut four strips of emery paper about ⅜″ wide. Beginning at the bottom edge of the roof, lay the strips lengthwise, overlapping them 1/16″.

Barn and house roofs were made from toothpaste tubes, cut open and flattened.

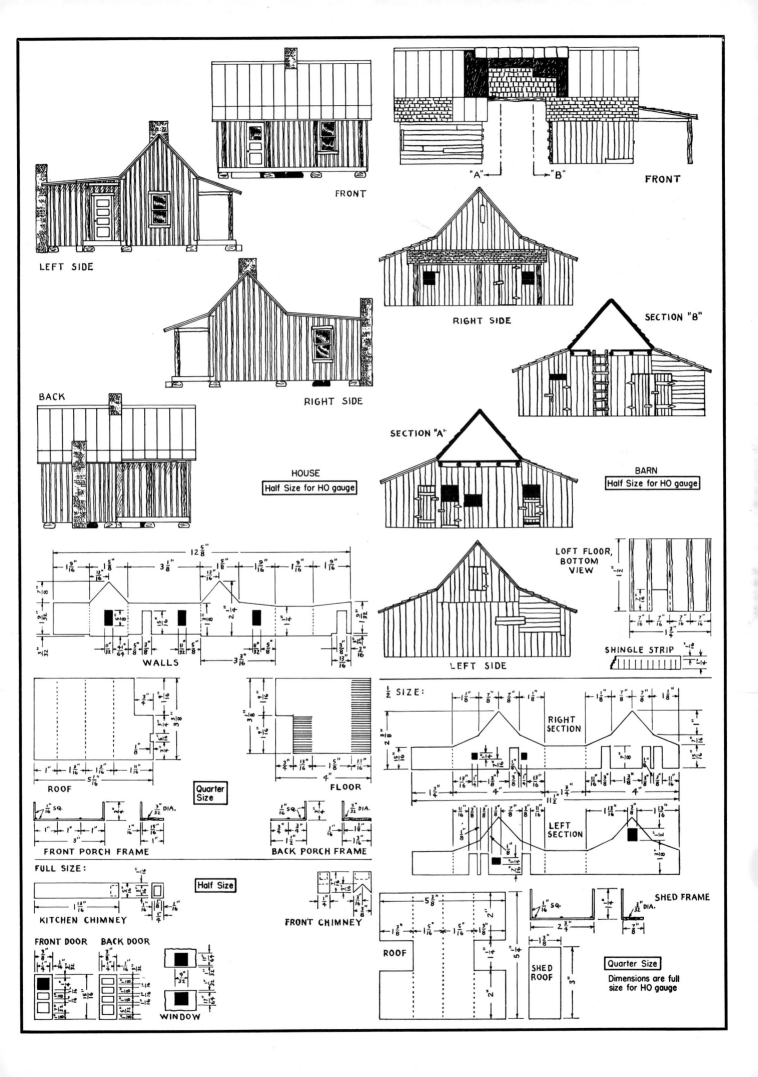

FRONT

LEFT SIDE

BACK

RIGHT SIDE

HOUSE
Half Size for HO gauge

FRONT

RIGHT SIDE

SECTION "B"

SECTION "A"

BARN
Half Size for HO gauge

LEFT SIDE

LOFT FLOOR, BOTTOM VIEW

SHINGLE STRIP

WALLS

ROOF

FLOOR

Quarter Size

FRONT PORCH FRAME

BACK PORCH FRAME

½ SIZE:

RIGHT SECTION

LEFT SECTION

SHED FRAME

ROOF

SHED ROOF

Quarter Size

Dimensions are full size for HO gauge

FULL SIZE:

KITCHEN CHIMNEY

Half Size

FRONT CHIMNEY

FRONT DOOR   BACK DOOR

WINDOW

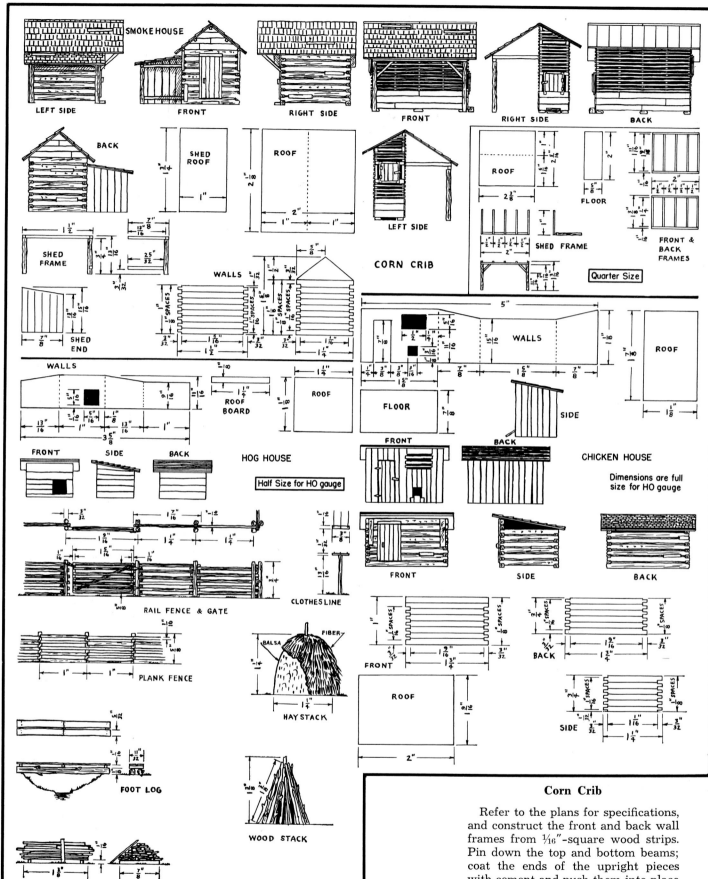

Hog House

Cut out the walls and scribe horizontal lines to indicate boards. Fold the walls, cement the edges together and brace them inside. When the

Bristol board roof is in position, cut about ten ⅛″ x 1¼″ boards from index card and cover the roof, overlapping them about ¹⁄₃₂″. Don't paint any buildings until all are finished.

Corn Crib

Refer to the plans for specifications, and construct the front and back wall frames from ¹⁄₁₆″-square wood strips. Pin down the top and bottom beams; coat the ends of the upright pieces with cement and push them into place between the beams.

Cut illustration board planks about ⅛″ wide and attach them to the lower part of the frame, allowing the bottom plank to extend ¹⁄₁₆″ below the bottom beam. Cover the frame with planks to a height of ⅜″. From illustration board, cut a number of strips 1/32″ wide and 2″ long. Cover the frames above the planks with these strips, spacing them about 1/32″ apart.

Make the floor of 1/16″ sheet balsa and cement the two completed walls to the top of it. Join the walls at the ends with a 1/16″-square slanting crosspiece at the top and with a horizontal crosspiece at the level of the back wall and another at the floor.

Cut two doors, 3/8″ square, from illustration board and score for planks. Cement a framework of 1/16″ illustration board strips, with an opening slightly smaller than the doors, to either side of the building. Attach the doors to the framework and add hinges and latches. Cover the rest of the sides with boards and laths as you did the front and back.

Whittle six balsa foundation stones 3/16″ square and 1/16″ thick; cement the rafters to the top of the beam. Turn this framework upside down and secure a rough post to either end of the beam. Add braces from beam to posts. Coat the ends of the rafters with cement and attach the frame to the front wall of the crib.

Cut the roof from heavy Bristol board and cement it to the crib. Following previous instructions, cover the front of the roof with shingles and the back with tin.

Smokehouse

The smokehouse is a hewn log building with an attached woodshed. After studying the plans, draw the four main walls on 3/32″ balsa wood. Mark lines 1/8″ apart on each wall. These spaces will represent the logs. With a sharp knife, cut out the walls. Cut notches 1/16″ wide and 3/32″ deep, centered on the 1/8″ spaced lines, in the edges of each piece. Make deep grooves along the 1/8″ spaced lines. Roughen the logs with a sharp point and patch the walls with illustration board planks. On the triangular part of the front and back walls, scribe lines to represent boards.

Cement a 3/8″ x 7/8″ index card door to the front wall; frame it with 1/16″ strips and use a bit of wood for a handle. Make a step of 1/16″ x 1/8″ balsa.

Check to see that the notches fit. Then cement the four log walls together. The side walls do not touch the ground.

The woodshed framework is similar to the porch and shed frames already described, except that it has two crosspieces at the back. Connect the frame to the wall of the smokehouse.

Cut the back wall of the woodshed from illustration board and divide it into planks. Cement it to the back of the frame and the corner of the smokehouse. Use heavy Bristol board for the shed roof and the main roof, attaching the shed roof first.

When the main roof is in place, cut five 1/16″ stripwood beams 1/2″ long and cement them to the underside of the overhang at the front of the building. Add the two diagonal braces. Cover the roof with shingles.

Spring House

Since it has hewn log walls of 3/32″ sheet balsa and a shingle roof, the spring house is built as the smokehouse was. In making the front wall, notice that the top log is not notched and is presumably held in place by boards. The door is 3/8″ x 3/4″.

Painting

The farmhouse should look as if it were whitewashed once. To achieve this effect, give the walls a coat of very thin black followed by a coat of thin white, splotched and mottled, varying from plank to plank. Use more thin black after this, especially at the bottom of walls.

Paint all tin roofs a thin, rusty reddish brown, and then spot and streak them with a thicker rust color. Vary the texture of tarpaper roofs by spots of dark gray.

All buildings except the house are a weathered gray; some can be of a darker hue. To paint a building, cover the entire structure, including shingle roofs, with thin black. Then paint individual boards, logs and shingles again, adding touches of brown. Indicate knotholes with dots of paint. Touch the bottoms of walls and also the roof of the spring house with green for moss.

In arranging the buildings on your layout, place the smokehouse just behind the house and locate the corn crib near the barn. Put the spring house above, or upstream, from the other buildings. The scene will be more interesting if the land is eroded, covered with weeds and dotted with stumps and rocks. Scatter a few shade trees about and, if you wish, plant a row or two of fruit trees.

Let a shallow stream run from the spring house. The stream may widen into a pond held back by an earth dam. For the pond, use a piece of glass painted greenish brown on the bottom and daubed with clear varnish on top.

When the buildings are in place, you may have room for other items. You will certainly want a barnyard fence and a hog pen.

The barnyard fence can be made of split rails laid between a double row of posts. Use some round posts, some roughly square, and some split. Make about 22 posts 3/4″ high for each actual foot of fence. Make the rails 1 7/16″ long, from 1/16″ square stripwood carved to a roughly triangular cross section, or else cut them from sheet wood. About 50 rails per foot are required.

If the landscape is hilly, it is best to build the fence right on the layout. With a sharp tool, such as an awl, punch depressions, with 1 1/4″ spacing, into the plaster base. Cement a post in each depression. Some work will be avoided if the fence is carried to the corners of the buildings.

Smear a rail with cement and lay it on the ground beside two posts. Skip a space and lay another rail and continue around the yard. Stack the next line of rails on this alternating row. Add rails until each section is about five rails high. At buildings and gates, space the rails with short blocks. Add the second row of posts so that the rails are stacked between two posts. Three posts are required at corners.

Construct gates with 1/32″ x 1/16″ stripwood frames covered with illustration board slats. Fasten the gates to posts with index card hinges and close them with loops of thread or scale chain.

A plank fence for the hog pen is similar to the rail fence, except that only one row of posts is needed. Use illustration board planks. Paint the fences a weathered gray.

To bridge the creek, cut two twigs or dowels, connect them with crosspieces and cover with illustration board planks. Make a pile of odd lumber by cementing scraps of stripwood and illustration board together.

To make a haystack, whittle a 1 1/4″ balsa cube to a hemispherical shape, coat it with cement and stick on something like hay, such as weather-stripping fiber or brown and tan yarn.

Cut 1/4″ lengths of stove wood and 3/8″ logs and pile them in the woodshed part of the smokehouse. Behind the woodshed, stack twigs to represent a pyramid of seasoning firewood.

Make a clothesline with round posts, 1/32″ x 1/16″ crosspieces, and thread. Hang tissue paper sheets and towels on the lines.

The detailing of your farm may be as extensive as you like. Make hoes, spades and pitchforks from wire and bits of metal. Hang short lengths of chain and coils of thread rope on walls.

At your dealer or in catalogs you will find numerous farm accessories such as tools, milk cans, barrels, pumps, tubs, chairs and ladders. Of course you also need people and animals. Almost any animal from a chicken to a draft horse is available commercially in HO and O scale.

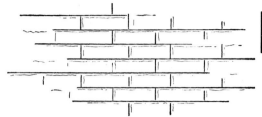

PUBLIC WAREHOUSE

BY JOE WILHELM

Photos by the author

WAREHOUSES are usually large, bulky buildings ill-suited to model railroad use, but here is one that is different. Just about all of us have sidings that angle out from the main line or other track, leaving very little space in the wedge-shaped piece of land that is formed. This warehouse, which was copied directly from a real one, was designed for just such a situation.

The prototype building has several odd things about it that serve to make it all the more interesting. The first floor has wood siding and the upper story is brick. The brick rests on large I-beams. There is a large door in the upper wall for lowering material into open cars, but it appears to be no longer in use. Some of the windows are boarded up. The office is located on the second floor at the wide end of the building; it is reached through the

doorway which doesn't have a door.

The smaller freight door in the end is used for loading trucks. The structure is painted a rather dark green, except for the brick and the light gray concrete. The metal fittings, such as the sill and the strap, are black. Lettering on the mainline side can be white on black or black on white.

Fig. 1 shows three sides of the building; Fig. 1A on page 88 shows the fourth side. Begin by cutting the four sides from poster board. Mark off the doors and windows. Draw vertical lines on the sides to denote the steel I-beams; they will be represented by making the brick and the wood of a piece of three-ply Bristol board and leaving a space sunken in to denote the beam. Paint the brick portion a solid brick color rather streaked with a bit of black. Make sure you use flat paint. Use white ink

to make the mortar lines for the brick side; I found Johnson's or Pelican drawing ink best for this. Do not draw these mortar lines all over the bricked surface, unless perhaps you are working in O gauge. Just a suggestion of the mortar lines is enough, as is shown in the drawing. Use a draftsman's ruling pen to do this; if you haven't one, I'd suggest that you buy yourself one. The ruling pen is fairly cheap and most necessary for countless modeling jobs.

Paint the 12" boards for the first floor a dark green; they are laid on one by one, but you could draw the lines with black ink on a sheet of three-ply Bristol. Cut out the doors before painting.

Cut the base from poster board and paint it a light gray to look like concrete. The steel reinforcements at the top edge of the foundation, and the

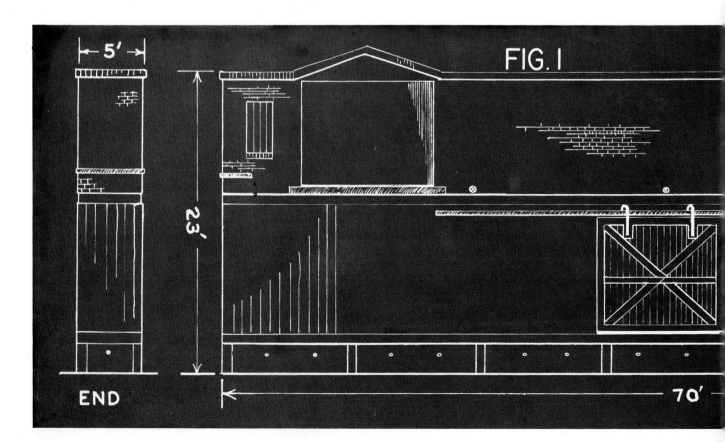

The idea for this warehouse came from an actual building designed to fit into a wedge-shaped plot of ground. It's wider at one end than at the other, and just right for the location at which a siding takes off from the main line.

ones running from the ground up at intervals, are painted green. Make them of two-ply Bristol. The bolt heads showing in the concrete part of the foundation are the ends of rods which hold the foundation together.

There is a peaked roof effect over the corrugated iron door in the second story. This is on one side only. The windows in the storage end of the prototype are boarded up with plain unpainted boards. Notice the iron strap at the narrow end of the building; don't forget to put this on your warehouse. It is shown in detail, as is the iron door, in Fig. 7 on page 89.

In Fig. 1, the view of the wider end of the building shows the position of the drainpipe, windows, and sliding door. The stairs lead to the open doorway, which in turn leads up a flight of

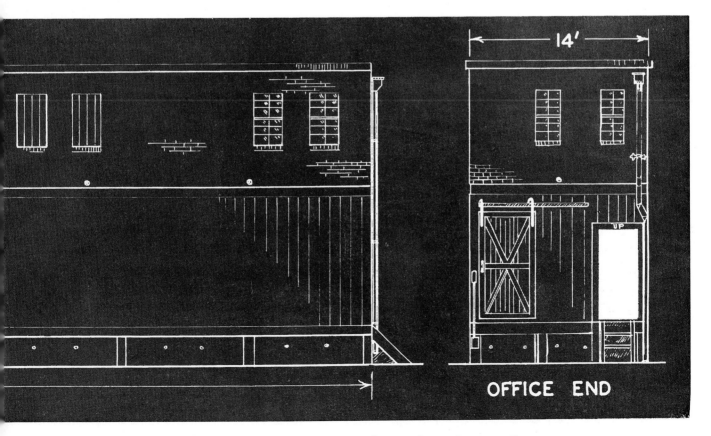

OFFICE END

FIG. 1A

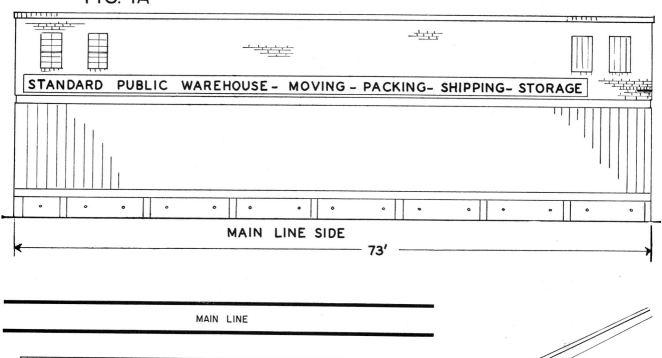

STANDARD PUBLIC WAREHOUSE - MOVING - PACKING - SHIPPING - STORAGE

MAIN LINE SIDE

73'

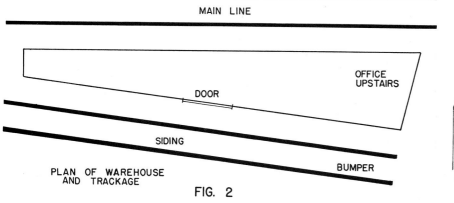

MAIN LINE

OFFICE
UPSTAIRS

DOOR

SIDING

BUMPER

PLAN OF WAREHOUSE
AND TRACKAGE

FIG. 2

GLUE SANDPAPER TO ROOF   FIG. 3

MAKING GRAVEL AND
TAR ROOF

You won't find this structure too hard to construct, for there are only a few windows, and some of them are boarded up! Working doors can be made without much trouble, too. Because the building is old, mortar lines do not show up well on the brick section; you can draw a few in as shown above.

stairs to the office. The electrical box is mounted next to the sliding door and should be painted silver, as noted in Fig. 7.

Fig. 2 shows a bird's-eye view of the setup. Note how close the main line is to the structure; no wonder there are no doors on that side! Don't forget to put a bumper at the end of the siding. Also, put a mark of some sort on the building or on the ground to show where a car should be spotted so the door will be in the right position for unloading.

The roof, which is below the level of the brickline, is of tar-and-gravel construction. This is very easy to simulate by the use of sandpaper; after the paper is attached, stain it with a wash of brown paint. (All paint and stains that you use should be flat; I suggest the use of colors ground in japan mixed with turpentine. They dry very fast and are perfectly flat.) Fig. 3 shows how the sandpaper fits on the roof.

Fig. 4 shows the window construction for the different types that are found in the building. There is nothing unusual about them, but you will

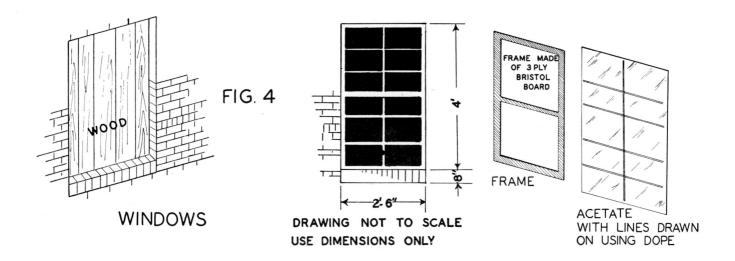

FIG. 4

WINDOWS

4'

8'

2'-6"

DRAWING NOT TO SCALE
USE DIMENSIONS ONLY

FRAME MADE
OF 3 PLY
BRISTOL
BOARD

FRAME

ACETATE
WITH LINES DRAWN
ON USING DOPE

find the boarded-up windows very easy to make compared with the regular type.

Fig. 5 shows a detail view of the construction of the sides; note the roof line. The row of bricks around the very top is put on with another layer of poster board. The bricks on this are up and down, as they are under the windows. You can get a good idea of the concrete foundation and iron construction from this drawing.

The doors, which are one of the most interesting features, are the subject of Fig. 6. Door slides are made of sheet brass. You can easily make a working door by simply hanging it from the runner, but if you don't care to include this feature, attach each door so it simply goes on or comes off. Then you can hang it in either a closed or open position.

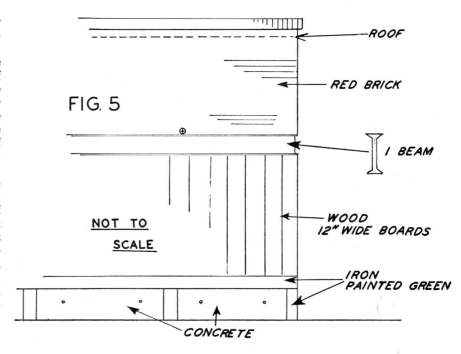

FIG. 5

NOT TO SCALE

ROOF

RED BRICK

I BEAM

WOOD
12" WIDE BOARDS

IRON
PAINTED GREEN

CONCRETE

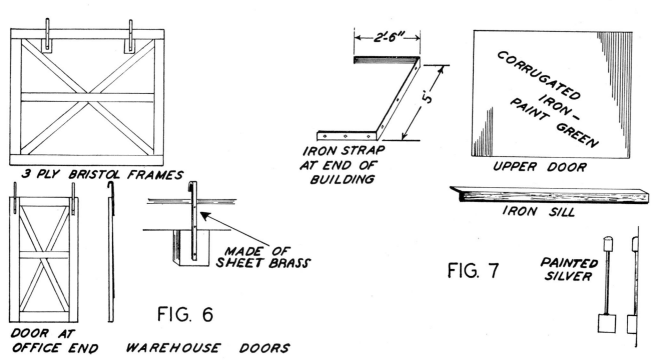

3 PLY BRISTOL FRAMES

DOOR AT
OFFICE END

WAREHOUSE DOORS

FIG. 6

MADE OF
SHEET BRASS

2'-6"

5'

IRON STRAP
AT END OF
BUILDING

CORRUGATED IRON-
PAINT GREEN

UPPER DOOR

IRON SILL

FIG. 7

PAINTED
SILVER

You'll seldom find a general store deserted, so be sure to put a few of the town characters at the one on your pike.

YOU'LL NEED CRACKER BARRELS AND CRANBERRY TUBS

A country general store

BY RAYMOND OVRESAT

JUST after you cross the old wooden bridge on the Slew River, take county road A to the right and go up it for about a mile. Then you'll see it — the general store. Sure you can get eggs there; horse harnesses, too, if you want. The Clarks handle about anything and everything. It doesn't look like much on the outside though, except for a bunch of signs, but inside you've got to be a regular Davy Crockett to get to the counter. You might stumble over several cracker barrels and cranberry tubs en route. You have to be careful of those rabbit traps and feedbags in the aisle, too. But don't worry if you knock something over; the Clarks have learned to pity us poor city ginks.

The Clarks' store is a typical one, just like most of the others in Beaver County — except those at the county seat. Just about all the towns in the county grew up around the local store. In fact, except for the houses and

church, there's not much more to the villages than the store, unless you count all the lopsided sheds you see. There are lots of those around.

Your pike needs at least one village like this, and you might as well begin with the general store.

Grab yourself a scale pile of clapboard siding, some 2 x 4's, a keg of nails, and a few rolls of tar paper. It's not so important that you model your store just like the one in the photographs. You'll have a lot more fun if you model a store you might have seen along the road on your Sunday afternoon travels. But, if you haven't seen any you want to model, the Clarks will be flattered if you choose theirs.

When you look over the photos, watch for the things that give individual character to what might otherwise

be a mere shell. Things like the sagging roof, rougher-than-usual clapboard siding, the multitude of signs and porch clutter, the way the false front reaches above the peaked roof. I'll try to tell you how to add this "finishing veneer" that gives the character and feeling you look for in a structure.

The Clarks' store measures 27 x 50 feet, excluding the shed in the rear. The height is 24 feet at the roof ridge and 27 feet at the front wall. No scale elevations are included, but you can get an idea of most of the measurements from the scale in the photo on page 92. Exact measurements are not important. If it looks right to you, that's all that counts.

Take a look at the construction drawing before you start. It will give you a better idea of how this thing will be tackled and will often be referred to. Building techniques might not follow prototype methods, but they'll suit your purposes better and the final results will be the same.

Walls

Make the four walls and roof of heavy cardboard. A good grade of illustration board about 1/16" thick is best. Since the front wall rises above the roof line, it is not solid. Cut the lower portion out of cardboard and build up the rest later. Locate the door and window openings as they occur on your prototype and cut them out of the wall pieces. Glue the walls together, bracing the corners and sides to prevent warping. Glue on the roof, and any additions there might be. The shell of the general store is then complete.

Now dress up the shell to make it look like something other than a refugee from a shoe-box factory. A logical starting place is the walls, and a logical covering for the walls is clapboard siding. Vertical siding with narrow battens sealing every board joint is sometimes used, but the clapboard is preferred. It can be put up by using wide or narrow boards, so take your choice.

Cut the siding from heavy file card

Most general stores have a shed of one kind or another at the rear. Don't be too particular in modeling it, because often they are sagging additions.

stock or manila folders, which are about the right weight of material. If the stock is too thick, it's difficult to cut; if too thin, it casts no shadow and has no relief. The individual strips should average a scale 6" in width.

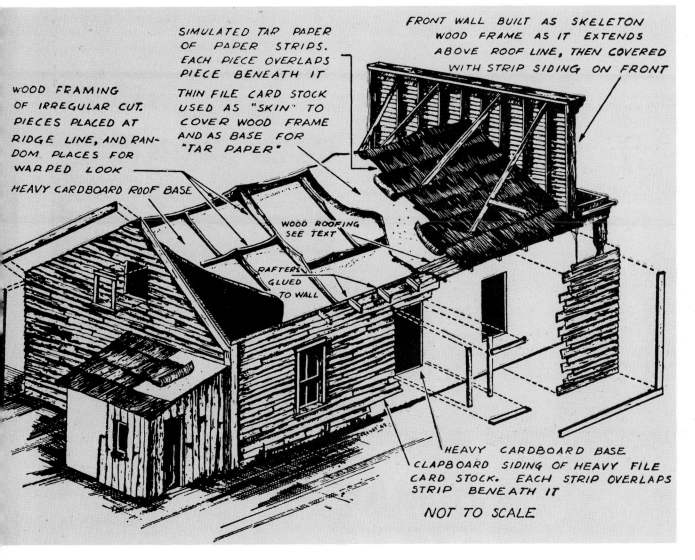

SIMULATED TAR PAPER OF PAPER STRIPS. EACH PIECE OVERLAPS PIECE BENEATH IT

THIN FILE CARD STOCK USED AS "SKIN" TO COVER WOOD FRAME AND AS BASE FOR "TAR PAPER"

FRONT WALL BUILT AS SKELETON WOOD FRAME AS IT EXTENDS ABOVE ROOF LINE, THEN COVERED WITH STRIP SIDING ON FRONT

WOOD FRAMING OF IRREGULAR CUT PIECES PLACED AT RIDGE LINE, AND RANDOM PLACES FOR WARPED LOOK

HEAVY CARDBOARD ROOF BASE

WOOD ROOFING SEE TEXT

RAFTERS GLUED TO WALL

HEAVY CARDBOARD BASE
CLAPBOARD SIDING OF HEAVY FILE CARD STOCK. EACH STRIP OVERLAPS STRIP BENEATH IT

NOT TO SCALE

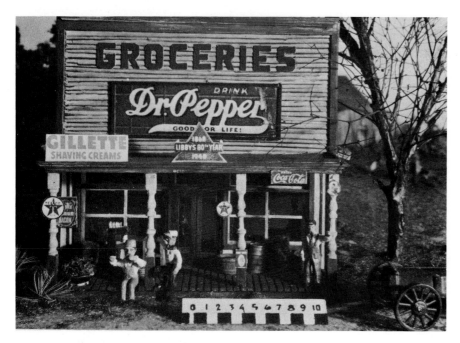

The scale rule will give you some idea of the measurements of the store. Signs can be cut from magazines or from match covers. Dirty them up a little and weather the sides so your model will be more in keeping with its era.

When your siding is ready, begin gluing it in place, mass-production fashion. Put an area of glue on the cardboard base and put the strips in place, starting at the bottom of the wall and working up. Let each strip overlap the one beneath it so about a scale 3" width is left exposed. Place some of the strips crooked so that the wall won't look too new nor perfect. You can glue the strips right over the window openings, for the openings can later be made easily with a razor blade. Keep the vertical joints at reasonable lengths.

In case your prototype has a false front, such as the Clarks' store, you'd better put it up now. The vertical framing is of scale 2 x 4's, doubled at the ends and topped with suitable horizontal members. According to actual practice they should be spaced 16" apart, but in HO 3 feet seems to look about right. Cover the front side of this frame as you did the other wall areas, being a little more careful with your gluing. The trim and paint details will come later.

Now you can put in window and door sashes. Make the doors of bass-wood pieces or a few layers of card. Set the paneling back from the face of the door. Make the window sashes in one piece, or two sets if you use common double-hung windows. Cut out the window sashes of card stock so that about a scale 2" of the sash shows around the edges. The same

2" should also show on any horizontal or vertical bars between panes.

The show windows in front of a general store are nothing much, most often not a single sheet of glass, but several panes. Glue the sashes in place as you finish them, but don't put any celluloid or glass in back of them for a while yet. It's better to do the painting before you complete these details.

Roof

The roof with the "old look" is next. Take a second glance at the construction drawing before you start it. You already have the heavy cardboard base, so now make the wood framing. Use balsa or basswood for the framing and cut out the ridge piece first in any shape that suits your fancy (or local weather conditions). Be sure to have the ridge rest atop it, supporting members where it meets the end walls so the roof will never fall there. You can build up the wall to that extra height by bringing the trim pieces of the back wall up to meet the height of the ridge piece, thus preventing any unsightly aperture.

After the ridge piece has been glued in place, cut out the "warped" rafters as you think they'll be needed to give the roof the right contour, and glue them in place. Cover the framework with sections cut from lightweight file-card stock. Apply glue liberally to the wood pieces and hold the sections in place for a few minutes until the glue has set.

Scrape the glue off your fingers and proceed with the business of the visible rafters and wood roofing. The idea is that wherever the roof extends beyond the limits of the wall, there should be visible roof boards and, alongside the side walls, rafters at regular intervals.

Instead of using individual boards this time, scribe the roof boards on a sheet of basswood. Cut out a piece, leaving about a scale foot for the overhang and another ⅜" so that the piece may be glued onto the roof you just finished. The change in surface will be covered by the tar paper. Turn the model on its back and glue the rafters in place. Space them the same as you did the verticals along the front wall.

Now cut out paper strips for the tar paper and glue them in place. Add narrow strips of wood at the edges of the roof to channel the water down in a few places instead of having a regular waterfall. While on the roof you can put up the chimney. The brick portion can be carved from balsa; so can the portion funneling up to the dowel used for the pipe. The flashing around the base can be made from card stock. You might as well paint everything at the same time, so hold

Visible roof boards and rafters should show where the roof extends beyond the limits of the wall. Don't forget to add braces to the false front after the roof is up. You can build the porch separately, then glue it in place.

off on the roof and chimney for a little while.

Now for the trim, including the porch if you're going to have one on your model. Basswood is good for the trim around the doors and windows. You can buy it in just the right size, about a scale 4" wide by 1" thick. No need cutting out extra strips. Remember, the window sills should project out from the side trim. Glue the pieces right over the clapboard siding. When the whole thing is painted, any unsightly joints will be covered. The trim at the corners and near the base can be made either of basswood, about 6" to 8" wide, or strips of heavy card stock. The front wall of the Clarks' store is topped off with a piece of gutter stock. The lower part of the front wall is practically made up of show windows, and you might want to get extra fancy with your woodwork details there.

Porch

The porch isn't a must, but it's very typical of most general stores, especially in places where the prairie sun would soon make the brightest calico rather sad looking. The porch adds interest too, and gives some extra posts on which to hang signs. Checker games can go on uninterrupted, come rain or shine.

Build the porch as a separate unit so that both the building and it can be more easily painted. After the paint is dry, the porch can be glued on. The porch floor can be solid or of typical boardwalk construction, with spaces between the boards for drainage. Strips of basswood scaled to your gauge will do the trick.

The posts can either be carved or plain. Those at the Clarks' store were made from carved stock sold as stanchions for ship models. They come in a wide variety of sizes and are ideal for posts and many other model parts. Only the middle sections of the posts were made from this stock. Square shafts were then glued on the top and bottom. Numerous designs are possible.

The porch roof is a flat piece of cardboard, and the cornice work around it is built of layers of basswood. You can get as ornate as you like on these porches, and somewhere you'll find a prototype that matches pretty closely. The sign man will be on the job soon, and so will the old busybodies you see out front. Oops, pardon!—the one on the right in the photos is Mr. Clark himself.

Painting

Everything is ready for painting, now, so get out your assortment of brushes and other painting gear. Paint the walls first. Mix a batch of poster color in a gray or brown color range. Apply the paint as thin as possible,

Douglas Bristow.

Douglas Bristow of Winston-Salem, N. C., built this general store for his Southern Piedmont Lines. He used discarded file folders and got his signs from magazines. The siding was put on from the bottom up, painted with water colors and rubbed to give it a weathered look. The figures and food were carved from bars of soap. Mr. Shermer is an up-to-date fellow: he has TV!

just so it will cover and won't clog. Cover the trim and all. After this first coat has dried, go over the wall again with various shades of the same color in lighter and darker tones, hitting some boards with the light and others with the dark, thereby establishing a more interesting over-all color. Look at any painted wall that's weathered a lot and see how many color variations it has. Use a clean damp brush to blend the values into each other if they get a little too spotty. It's a good idea, too, especially in HO gauge, to emphasize occasional board joints with India ink.

After all the walls have been done, you can go around with the trim color. Paint the doors and windows on this trip, too, using either color. Save a little of each color for touch-up work.

Back up to the roof now. Use black poster paint for it, keeping it thin so that it won't streak. The poster color will dry a flat bluish black that's fine on looks. Then seal up the joints using black airplane dope. Put it on thick. Use it for the chimney flashing, metal funnel and pipe too. After the dope has dried, its glossy appearance can be toned down considerably and realistically by brushing black poster paint on it. The paint will adhere reluctantly to the dope and the resulting appearance is of a spotty and dusty film, doing away with that shiny newness entirely. The chimney brick

can be simulated with poster color.

Now that the roof is finished, glue the supports for the upper front wall in place and paint them. The celluloid can be put in place in back of the window. Green window shades can be added, too, if you like. The porch can be glued on now, just about finishing the building except for a little atmosphere in the form of signs, barrels, boxes and a few old geezers out front to keep tab on the customers.

The signs that cover a good part of the Clarks' store were cut from magazines, newspapers and match covers. Only the "Groceries" sign on top was made from scratch. The Coca-Cola sign on the side was dirtied before being framed and erected. The lettering "Groceries" beneath it was done on the typewriter.

Select signs that are in scale and colorful; they add a lot to the structure. Various items, such as the milk can, barrel, tub and scale, can be purchased. The figures can be purchased cheaply and in a variety of positions. Paint them as accurately as your patience permits. With this all done, scoop out a little plot alongside your tracks for the store. Let the trees and scrub grass grow where they may and let the old boys glare out at you from the porch. Maybe someone will move in across the street. Town's liable to grow, you know, especially now that you have a general store.

BY EUGENE LE DOUX
Photos by the author

ALTHOUGH almost all of the railroads in the country have either eliminated or drastically cut their own coal requirements, they must continue to serve the many other consumers of this commodity. That's reason enough to install a coal yard on any type of layout, whether the pike is strictly diesel or not.

The prototype for Macy's coal yard is on a bank of the Genesee River, on the south side of the city of Rochester, N. Y. Like many other railroads, the

one which supplies this coal yard runs parallel to the river for some distance. The reason railroads do this is that the land alongside a river is usually quite level; that makes the job of track-laying much easier for the railroads' construction crews.

I followed the prototype closely in making my model, and only the name of the yard has been changed to prevent free advertising!

I would be exaggerating if I said the material used in making this model

cost more than 15 cents. Here's a complete list of what you will need:

Cardboard — thick and thin.
Stripwood: ⅛" square and ³⁄₃₂" square (for HO).
Paper tape.
India ink.
Black thread.
Mailing tube (or wax paper or towel tube).
Wire.
Scribed wood (optional).

Put them all together and you'll have

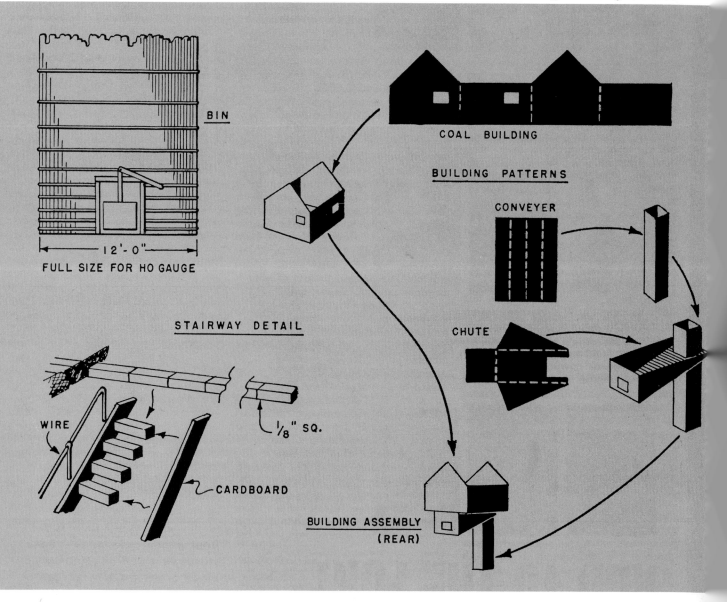

BIN

FULL SIZE FOR HO GAUGE

|← 12'-0" →|

COAL BUILDING

BUILDING PATTERNS

CONVEYER

CHUTE

STAIRWAY DETAIL

WIRE

⅛" SQ.

CARDBOARD

BUILDING ASSEMBLY
(REAR)

Men at work liven up this scene at Macy's coal yard on Eugene Le Doux's pike. This is a good structure for a railroad, which hauls coal to supply the yard.

a coal yard. Here is how it's done:

Like Horatio Alger, start at the bottom and work your way up. The base is made primarily from stripwood. Brace the ⅛"-square corner posts with the ³⁄₃₂"-square vertical beams. Also, glue two pairs of diagonal braces, made from card stock, on the left and right sides of the base framework. The front and rear sides of the base do not have diagonal braces since they would interfere with the chutes which enter and leave the building. To make the stairway under the building, simply cut a sufficient number of stripwood pieces about 2 scale feet in length. Next, glue the ends of these steps to two narrow pieces of cardboard to form a stairway. See the stairway detail at the left, and plans on next page.

The building itself is made almost entirely of cardboard. The two exceptions are the wire for the railing on the stairway and the paper tape which is used to simulate a tarpaper roof. Use the India ink to scribe the

sides of the building. However, you could use commercial scribed wood instead of drawing the boards on with ink. I did not use it because the scribes appeared too straight and uniform to suit my purposes. I wanted my model to appear as a weather-beaten time-worn structure, somewhat dilapidated like the prototype. So I drew the boards on the heavy card stock free-hand, thus eliminating the possibility of uniformity which might have occurred if I had used a ruler. I would advise you to spend a little more time on this part of the construction since the scribing appears on more than three fourths of the model.

After you have settled the scribing problem, go ahead and cut out all of the sides for the coal building and for the chutes. The patterns for these parts are all shown on the opposite

page. After you have cut them out, scribe them if necessary, glue them together, and then attach the roof which has been covered with "tar-paper" tape.

I used dark brown cardboard to make the sides of my building so all I had to do at this point was smear a little coal-dust mixture on the structure. However, if you have to paint your model, don't forget to smear it afterward. Colored pastels, similar to chalk, are available in any artists' supply store and they make excellent "smearing" mixtures.

I used scribed wood for the sides of the bin because, as I think you'll agree, it has all the advantages. Glue the scribed wood around a mailing tube or a reasonable facsimile. Black thread retaining bands help to hold the old boards of the bin together. Cut irregular notches in the top rim of the bin so that it appears worn and battered by years of wear. Notice the small chute door at the base of the bin; it is made from scrap wood and cardboard. Paint the entire bin a dark brownish-black, the same color as the coal building.

To dress up (dress down would be more like it, because coal yards are rarely if ever dressed-up), don't forget to add the little extra details that are the mark of a "terrific" layout. Here are some suggestions for details that you might use:

(1) A coal conveyer, such as the one made by Dyna-Model, which carries coal from the bin to a coal truck.

(2) A coal truck (Dyna-Model).

(3) Coal in the bin and scattered around the yard, especially near the bin and under the chutes.

(4) People (Weston mini-figures and Dyna-Model figures).

(5) An office or shack; the boss has to keep the books somewhere!

(6) Perhaps a fence to enclose part of the yard; this is a common practice around coal yards.

(7) Signs cut from magazine advertisements and glued to the building.

All these details will make your coal yard look like a live-wire outfit, with lots of activity taking place.

The sides of the coal building give good display to advertisements. The coal conveyer and coal truck are almost essential equipment for the yard.

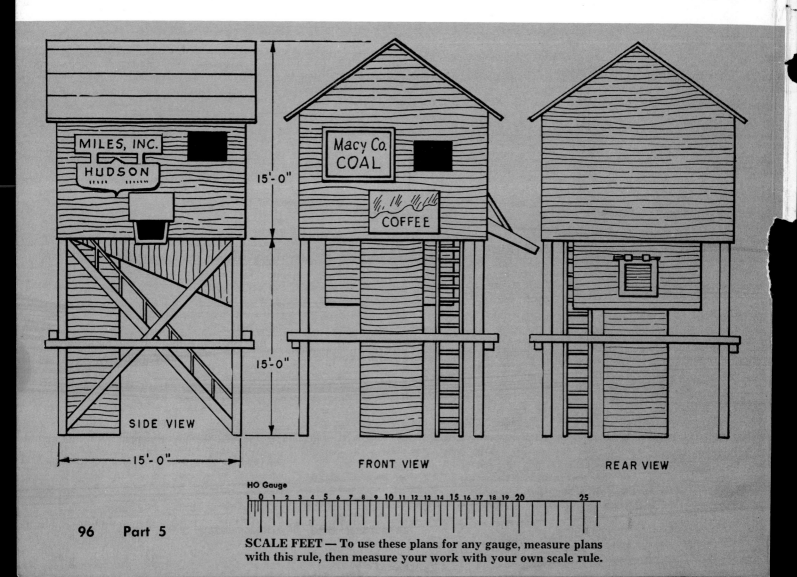

MILES, INC.

HUDSON

Macy Co. COAL

COFFEE

15'-0"

15'-0"

15'-0"

SIDE VIEW

FRONT VIEW

REAR VIEW

HO Gauge

0 1 2 3 4 5 6 7 8 9 10 11 12 13 14 15 16 17 18 19 20   25

SCALE FEET — To use these plans for any gauge, measure plans with this rule, then measure your work with your own scale rule.